# What Are They Saying About Peace and War?

*Thomas A. Shannon*

**PAULIST PRESS**
New York/Ramsey

*To my dear daughters,*
*Ashley and Courtney,*
*for whom I wish the gift of peace*

Library of Congress
Catalog Card Number: 82-60749

ISBN: 0-8091-2499-8

Published by Paulist Press
545 Island Road, Ramsey, N.J. 07446

Printed and bound in the
United States of America

# Contents

# Preface

Hammer your ploughshares into swords,
your sickles into spears             **(Joel 4:10).**

These will hammer their swords into ploughshares,
their spears into sickles             **(Isaiah 2:4).**

Such biblical ambivalence indicates only a small part of the dilemmas one encounters in trying to establish an ethical analysis of war. The contemporary tension was set out clearly by Pope John Paul II in his 1982 Day of Peace Message:

> This is why Christians, even as they strive to resist and prevent every form of warfare, have no hesitation in recalling that, in the name of an elementary requirement of justice, peoples have a right and even a duty to protect their existence and freedom by proportionate means against an unjust aggressor.

> . . . in view of the difference between classical warfare and nuclear or bacteriological wars—a difference so to speak of nature—and in view of the scandal of the arms race seen against the background of the needs of the third world, this right, which is very real in principle, only underlines the urgency for world society to equip itself with effective means of negotiation.

The tension between the right to self-defense and the dramatically changed nature of war constitutes the context in which the moral concerns about war are set forth. While I am concerned with the history of the just war theory, I am also concerned with the moral arguments about war which emerge out of the American context, especially in our day. A tremendous change is occurring in the moral analysis of war and I wish to capture that development in particular.

I hope that this presentation will help to illuminate many of the issues that are involved in the current discussion of the ethics of warfare and that it will make a contribution to the development of an American Catholic moral analysis of war.

# 1
# The Development of the Just War Tradition

## War and Ancient Cultures and Religions

It is a fact of history and of life that violence and war always seem to have been with us. From a biological point of view, there has always been the competition of species in which one species uses another for its food supply. This helped preserve the chain of life and, consequently, population stability was maintained and an ecological balance was preserved. What is unique, however, when we observe human behavior, is that, in stark contrast to the majority of animal species, humans kill each other, sometimes to gain food and land but also and uniquely for ideological reasons. We seem to be one of the few species of animal life which kills members of its own species. While other animals certainly battle to maintain territorial and sexual status, these ritual battles seldom result in the death of the opponents. For better or worse, human beings seem to be unique, not only with respect to their consciousness and language abilities, but also for their ability to engage in intraspecies killing.

In spite of this fact of the violence of our species, almost every culture and civilization has some type of postulation of a golden age in which all peoples lived in harmony. This hypothesized age can have a variety of forms but the basic belief is fairly constant: people lived in peace, shared what they had, and life was harmonious. Whether this golden age is a dim memory from the origins of our race, or whether it is simply an expression of deep longing of human

3

beings, it is nonetheless the case that such an age was not a reality, at least in the civilizations that we know of. It is certainly not the case at the present time. For better or worse, most religions of the ancient world, as well as contemporary religions, have found a way to justify or accommodate themselves to the reality of war.[1]

## Zoroastrianism

This mideastern religion, popular around the sixth century before our common era, used the metaphor of military battles to describe its main theological insight: life was a battle between the forces of light and the forces of darkness. This religion postulated an eschatological battle in which the forces of good were eventually to triumph. This religion also served to provide the ideological background for the growing nationalism underway in the ancient Persian empire. Zoroastrianism provided both a basis for ideological unity as well as the inspiration for the many and frequent wars that were fought during the expansion of the Persian empire.

For the Zoroastrians life was seen as a battle and, not unsurprisingly, this religion provided a basis for many of the polemics during the formation and expansion of the Persian empire.

## Hinduism

Hinduism is the traditional religion of India and among the most ancient of the world religions. One of its unique features is that it defined a specific warrior caste. The members of this caste had to live out their dharma (fate) by doing what was appropriate for their particular state in life. The military duties defined by membership in this caste transcended family obligations, and fidelity to them insured a favorable outcome to one's destiny.

Hinduism provided rules for the conduct of war. Members of a cavalry unit would fight only against other cavalry units; infantry could fight only against other infantry, and, in a foreshadowing of later theories of war, Hinduism mandated that the wounded, prisoners, runaways, and other non-combatants be treated in a respectful manner.

Hinduism did not allow all members of the religion to fight but it relegated that duty to one specific caste and assigned specific rules for the conduct of how war was to be carried out.

## Buddhism

The ancient religion of Buddhism, predominant in some areas of India, Japan, and China, had as the first of its five major precepts a prohibition on killing. This obligation was binding upon both the monks and the laity. For killing to be considered a sin, several conditions had to be simultaneously met: the one killed had to be, in fact, a living being; the person doing the killing had to know that this individual was a living being; there had to be an intent to kill; appropriate means had to be used (these included bare hands, orders to others, the use of weapons or other instruments, trapping, magic, or the forces of one's mind); finally, death had to actually occur. While these rules could be used in a casuistic fashion to justify some forms of killing as not being morally reprehensible, nonetheless, they indicate the seriousness with which the precept was taken and its significance within the religion.

Mahayana Buddhism, a liberal form of Buddhism developing approximately a century after the death of the Buddha, allowed several justifications for killing. Some of these have a very ironic modern ring to them. Killing was allowed to protect the purity of Buddhist doctrine. In an extreme situation, it was morally preferable to kill one person rather than have two individuals die. Finally, there was the perception that it was better to kill another person rather than to allow that person to kill someone else.

Thus, although there is in Buddhism a strong emphasis on not killing, openings began to be made and these provided the basis for an expansion of the justifications for killing which had a significant impact on the development of such justifications in other religions.

## Greece and Rome

In these two ancient civilizations peace was prized—in Greece as a state of order and coherence and in Rome as an agreement between parties not to fight. Nonetheless, both of these cultures were continuously and deeply involved in the enterprise of war. Although seen by the Stoics as irrational and contrary to the structure of the universe, nonetheless war was frequently waged, oftentimes to gain the harvest of the neighboring town or city or to conquer the known world, as was the case with Alexander. Rome also fought to extend its rule over the known world, although it attempted to do this through concessions and mediations as well as conquests. In both cultures there were gods and goddesses of peace as well as of war. The army was perceived to be both an army for waging war as well as a police force for ensuring domestic harmony.

Both of these empires relied upon their armies to ensure their rule throughout the known world, and then they relied upon them to maintain the order that they had secured. Peace was prized, but war was important and quite frequently the means to achieve the goal of peace. The legacy of Rome at the beginning of Christianity was the Pax Romana, but this was a peace forged through the waging of war and enforced through a standing army.

## Judaism

As a religion, Judaism was born in a slave rebellion and was established through a gradual process of the conquest of the people who occupied what was to become the ancient nation of Israel. Thus, one dimension of Judaism, especially reflected in many of its Scriptures, justified war and various battles as a way of fulfilling the mandate that Yahweh had given them to establish their own land. In many of these passages God is defined as a warrior and as one who directs battles and insures victory.

Yet there is another strand in Judaism in which the ideal of peace is presented. Many of these passages are found in the writings of prophets in which there is a looking forward to the messianic age when all of God's promises will be fulfilled and an age of peace will be established.

The rabbinic tradition distinguished two types of war: optional war and obligatory war. An optional war is basically a defensive war in which a nation will initiate a preemptive strike to avoid being attacked. The tradition did not easily justify this type of war and it was always suspect. The obligatory war was in response to an attack from the outside. The purpose of war here was to defend oneself, to protect one's home and homeland. Yet, even in this mandated war of defense, there were limits. Fruit trees, fields, and homes could not be destroyed. Women, especially those taken prisoner, were to be treated humanely. And the Jewish army could lay siege to a town only on three sides so that those who wished to escape could do so.

The Jewish tradition affirms the desirability of peace but also recognizes, especially in its historical circumstances, the necessity of war. While the tradition affirms the significance of peace and its desirability and eventual presence in the messianic kingdom, it also affirms the right of the people to defend themselves by repelling an enemy. Even here, however, the tradition recognizes that there must be limits in how one does this and in this way seeks to establish the seeds of peace even while fighting continues.

## Islam

One of the central concepts of Islam, the youngest of the world's major religions, is that of the Jihad: a striving in the way of God or a pursuit of the worship of God. The Jihad is the way in which the member of Islam lives out the obligation to submit totally to the rule of God in one's life. There is a military dimension to the Jihad which argues that it is appropriate to extend the rule of Islam through military means or to go to war against unbelievers or enemies of the faith. In this military sense, then, the Jihad functions as a justified religious war fought against polytheists, apostates, or some enemy of Islam. Its major purpose is to establish a universal theocratic state bound together in the worship of Allah, the one true God.

There are in Islam, like the other religions we have discussed, rules for the conduct of war. Primary among these is the rule that non-combatants are to be spared unless they are indirectly helping the cause of the enemy. The areas that can be destroyed are limited to those which cannot be brought under the political or military control of Islam. Also, animals are to be spared, although crops and inanimate objects can be destroyed. Interestingly enough in a desert country, the water supply can be destroyed or poisoned.

The concept of the Jihad in Islam is in many ways analogous to the concept of the crusade that we encounter in Christianity. It is a holy war fought against a religious enemy for the purpose of establishing the rule of God over all peoples.

## Jainism

The one major exception to the sanctioning of war and killing by the ancient religions and cultures is that of Jainism. Jainism is an offshoot of Hinduism and has continued to exist in a relatively pure form to the present day. Jainism focused on the doctrine of ahimsa: a renunciation of the will or desire to kill or harm any living organism. This was carried to its logical conclusion so that Jains were recognized by the gauze mask they wore over their mouths lest they accidentally breathe in and swallow an insect, their habit of sweeping the ground before them with a broom so that they would not step on any organism, and, in particular, by a steadfast refusal to kill any living being. Jains typically withdrew from the world, ate food prepared for them by others and obtained through begging, refused to practice agriculture, and would not engage in any type of violent activities. In a world of growing violence the Jains were conspicuous by their nonviolence and what could be characterized as a type of pacifism. Their vision provided the inspiration for Gandhi's philosophy of nonviolence. While many people argued that the Jains are irrelevant because of their lifestyle, they have at least had a significant impact upon civilization through inspiring a whole philosophy of nonviolence.

## Christianity

Like other major world religions, Christianity developed a position on war. The remaining sections of this chapter will sketch out different dimensions of this development.[2]

## The Early Community

Christianity began its development as a sect of Judaism. The early Christians maintained strong ties with the Jewish community and, in fact, continued to participate actively in Judaism. Only after the growing realization of the significance of the claim that Jesus was the Son of God did the split between the Christian and Jewish community begin to grow. Over the course of several decades, differences in theology, worship, and community organization helped the Christians develop their own autonomy and distinctiveness from Judaism.

Like many other peoples during this particular time period of history, the Christians were awaiting the end of the world. The specific content of this hope was focused around the imminent return of the resurrected and glorified Jesus. The early Christians assumed that Jesus would return, if not within their lifetime, certainly within the lifetime of their children. The first Christian community lived its life in the expectation that at any moment God's kingdom would break into their world and bring it and them to their fulfillment with God.

Because of this, Christians tended not to become involved in the life and structures of the community around them. Since they were awaiting the imminent return of Jesus, the needs of everyday life as well as the significance of social institutions took on less and less importance to them. While such an attitude may be difficult for us to understand in our present situation, nonetheless such an expectation of the imminent end of the world goes a long way to explaining why Christians focused on celibacy, why they did not participate in government and education, and why, often enough, they even quit their jobs. The extent of this withdrawal from the world can be seen in Paul's Second Letter to the Thessalonians in which he chides the Christian community at Thessalonica and requests that they return to work instead of sitting around, waiting for the world to end.

Christians were typically not involved in the affairs of the larger community around them. The early members of the Christian community were drawn from the lower socio-economic classes, and their marginal status helps explain why many more of them were not actively involved in the affairs of the empire. But more importantly, the early community perceived no religious social mandate to change the obvious inequities of the society around them. Without motivation to change what they saw, and seduced by their expectation of the end of the world, the Christians saw no gain in entering the structures of the world around them.

*The Changing Situation*

As a matter of very obvious fact, the world did not end within the first generation of the founding of Christianity. The delay of the second coming of Jesus constituted the first major crisis of faith within the early community. This crisis was resolved by affirming that Jesus would indeed return and bring the world to its heavenly consummation but that this would be at an unknown future time. Such an explanation was based on interpretations of some of the different parables, for example the one in which the Son of Man is described as coming like a thief in the night.

This delay meant that if Christians were to survive personally and socially, they could no longer remain exclusively within the confines of their community. And indeed Christians, once they realized that the world was not going to end, began to participate more and more in the affairs of the community around them. This turning outward on the part of the Christian community was also enhanced and somewhat necessitated because of the growth of the community and because of the presence of Christians in different socio-economic strata within the empire.

The fact of the continuation of the world, a growing community, and a much more economically mixed community brought about pressures for the Church to develop an ethic that would take this changed social situation into account. Once the faces of Christians were turned outward to the world instead of being focused on the heavens looking for the return of Jesus, it became apparent that they had to take into account the conditions in which they lived to determine how one might live as a Christian within the world. One important area of this development of a new Christian social ethic had to do with examining the reality of war.

*The Development of the Just War Theory*

(a) The Tradition of the Early Church

"From the end of the New Testament period to the decade A.D. 170–180 there is no evidence whatever of Christians in the army."[3] This statement by Roland Bainton is fairly well accepted. The problem is in trying to explain why this was the case. One explanation has to do undoubtedly with Christians' not typically joining in the structures of the larger society. Another reason is the slow growth of Christianity among those classes who were likely to be soldiers. Also, soldiers had to participate in the religious services of the empire which were considered idolatry by Christians. Finally, the Church had a rigoristic morality which uneasily readmitted to Communion people who committed apostasy, adultery, or bloodshed. The Christians were attempting to live out the love ethic of Jesus and such an ethic would, at least, *prima facie,* rule out the shedding of blood.

(b)  Participation in the Army and War

For some reason, the year 173 marks the turning point for participation of Christians in the military. Christians were in one of Marcus Aurelius' legions. Tertullian provides indirect evidence of the presence of Christians in the palace, the senate, the forum, and the army. During the persecution of Decius in 250 there is a reference to soldier martyrs. In 303, Galerius tried to eliminate Christians from his army. Christians seemed more likely to participate in war the closer they were to the frontiers of the empire. Finally, service in the army was legitimated because it also served as a type of police force.

These developments reflect a tension in the early Christian attitude toward war. On the one hand, there was a recognition that killing was at least, if not incompatible with Christianity, very difficult to justify. On the other hand, it became a growing practice for Christians to serve in the army. At times it was easy to argue against service to the empire by being a soldier because of the necessity of participating in idolatry or because the Roman army was the instrument through which the empire persecuted Christians. If love were the supreme value for Christians, then fighting and killing were difficult to justify. On the other hand though, as Christianity grew, soldiers also converted and there is no record of any requirement to resign. As the expectation of Jesus' imminent return began to lessen, Christians naturally gravitated toward available ways of making a living, and the army provided one of these. Then too, especially on the edges of the empire, there was a need to defend the empire against the skirmishes of the barbarians. Finally, the more the army took on the function of a police force, the less problematic service in that army became.

Nonetheless, the most significant circumstance which changed the tilt of the early Church toward pacifism or non-violence came from two external forces. The first was the unification of the Roman Empire under Constantine, one dimension of which was his making Christianity the official religion of the Roman Empire. In addition to having one faith, one Lord, and one baptism there was now one empire and one emperor. Such a situation allowed a significant assimilation of Christians into all dimensions of the life of the empire and gave Christianity a privileged position insofar as it was now the religion of the empire—a dramatic reversal from the persecutions only so recently experienced.

The second factor responsible for the change in orientation of Christianity toward war came as a result of the growing invasions of the so-called barbarians. The issue here, simply stated, was that since Christianity was now the religion of the empire, its survival was intimately bound up with the fate of the empire. The assumption was that if Christianity were to survive, so must the empire. Therefore when the fate of the empire was in jeopardy, it was appropriate to defend the empire so that Christianity might survive.

(c) The Ethical Justification of War in Christianity

### St. Ambrose

The first major ethic of war comes from Ambrose. Before being elected to the bishopric of Milan, Ambrose had been the pretorian prefect of northern Italy. He was thus no stranger to the army and to the purposes it could fulfill. These purposes became more apparent to him because of the invasion of the barbarians, especially since many of these barbarians were also bearers of various heresies, such as Arianism. By developing an ethic justifying war, the empire's boundaries could be maintained and even expanded and doctrinal purity could be enforced and new converts made.

Ambrose developed his Christian ethic of war from two sources. The first of these used the many military examples from the Jewish Scriptures adopted by the Christians. The campaigns conducted by the Jewish people in the conquest of the land of Canaan provided many examples which helped to justify Christian participation in war. Second, Ambrose adopted a Stoic ethic through his own reading of Cicero, especially the work *De Officiis,* in which Cicero developed a type of just war theory. Briefly stated, Cicero argued that the only cause of going to war was that we might live unharmed in a time of peace. When the victory was won, mercy should be shown to those who had lost. Also no war should be entered unless there had been an official demand for satisfaction given or a formal declaration made, following an appropriate warning. War could be entered to preserve the safety of a city, to protect the innocent, to avenge wrongs, and to honor pledges made to allies.

Ambrose adopted these elements for his theory of a just war, but he argued that those who were clerics should not participate in war. The image of clerics fighting in war seemed to be incompatible with the duty of their office which focused primarily on duties to the soul.

### Augustine

The major thrust for the full development of a Christian ethic of war came from Augustine, one of the most influential of all Catholic theologians. Again, Augustine's context is important in understanding his orientation toward war. Augustine was a classically trained Roman, familiar with the writings of the best philosophers of his age. He was also for many years a member of the Manichean religion, and much of his later life was spent in repenting these teachings. Also Augustine was a member of a mature Catholicism, one which was co-extensive with the empire and which now had a relatively clear tradition of its own, as well as a recognized center in Rome. Finally, Augustine lived in Africa, and Africa was in danger of being invaded by the Vandals. Only the Roman army stood between them and the destruction of the empire. All of these elements combined to persuade Augustine that order and the empire were preferable to chaos and that the survival of Christianity was tied up with the fate of the empire. Because the empire was Christian, the Church might be able to give some guidance and achieve some sense of justice. Therefore the empire could be defended and Christians could participate in that defense.

In his major work, *The City of God,* Augustine says, "A just war, moreover, is justified only by the injustice of an aggressor, and that injustice ought to be a source of grief to any good man, because it is human injustice."[4] This serves as the primary justification for declaring war and participating in it. Eventually in his other writings, Augustine added on other dimensions that were to serve as the framework for the development of the just war theory in Catholicism: it was to be waged only under the authority of the ruler; the conduct of the war must be just, and the clergy could not participate in war.

Augustine was not looking for the possibility of Christian perfection on earth. He recognized that injustice and war would be part of the reality of life in his age. On the other hand, he felt that Christianity should try to humanize war insofar as possible. He regarded peace as an ideal and tried to make the rules of war subservient to this end. In trying to restrain war, Augustine hoped that justice could be restored and that love could continue to be the dominant disposition that would rule the relationship between individuals. For Augustine, however, love was an interior attitude or disposition compatible with various actions, including killing an enemy out of the motive of love. Realism had entered Christianity.

### Thomas Aquinas

Because of the quality of his theological reflections and his status within the theological community, the thought of Aquinas had a most significant role in the development of traditional Roman Catholic theology. In his major work, the *Summa Theologica,* Aquinas provides a summary of his teaching on war.

> There are three conditions of a just war. First, the authority of the sovereign by whose command the war is to be waged. For it is not the business of the private individual to declare war or to summon the nation. The second condition is that hostility should begin because of some crime on the part of the enemy. Wherefore Augustine observes that a just war is wont to be described as one that avenges wrongs, when a nation or state has to be punished for refusing to make amends for the injuries done by its people or to restore what has been seized unjustly. The third condition is a rightful intention, the advancement of good or the avoidance of evil. It may happen that a war declared by a legitimate authority for a just cause may yet be rendered unlawful through a wicked intention. And Augustine declares that the passion of inflicting harm, the cruel thirst for vengeance, a plundering and implacable spirit, the fever

of turmoil, the lust for power and suchlike, all these are justly condemned in war.[5]

Aquinas also prohibits bishops and clergy from participating in war because their ministry is directed to the service of God. Thus, as in Augustine, the clergy are held to the norm of pacifism and may not rely on worldly weapons for their own defense.

## Summary

By the end of the thirteenth century, the major elements of the Christian ethic of war were in place. The Church had moved from a position of non-involvement and pacifism to a situation of significant involvement within the Roman Empire and society at large. This new situation included the possibility of engaging in the defense of that society. Part of this was done out of a sense that the empire was worth defending as a means of preserving Christianity and partly out of the sense that the Church could help to humanize the reality of war by making it a rule-governed activity. The basic criteria for conducting a just war at this period can be summarized as follows: war must be declared by the authority of the state; there must be a just cause; the intention must be just; war must be the last resort; only right means may be employed in the conduct of war; there must be a reasonable hope of victory; the good to be achieved must ouweigh the evils of war.

Christians were now to find themselves in a variety of situations in which they were able to participate in fighting. These ranged from the defense of the empire against the barbarians to the participation in the Crusades fought at the instigation of the Church and state to repel the Moslems from the Roman Empire and also to try to impose Christianity upon them. Such Crusades would be replicated in the various wars of religion that would devastate Christianity and Europe following the Reformation.

This tradition was also complemented by the assumption that citizens were basically to obey the command of the state to participate in war. This tradition and some of the motivations and justifications for it are exemplified nicely in the quote from the sixteenth century Spanish moral theologian Vitoria.

Other lesser folk who have no place or audience in the prince's counsel or in the public counsel are under no obligation to examine the causes of war but may serve in it in reliance on their betters. This is proved, first, by the fact that it is impossible and inexpedient to give reasons for all kinds of acts of state to every member of the commonalty. Also by the fact that men of the lower orders, even if they perceived the injustice of a war, could not stop it, and their voice would not be heeded. Therefore, any examination by them of the causes of a war would be futile. Also by the fact that for men of this sort it is enough proof of the justice of war (unless the contrary be quite certain) that it is being waged after public counsel and by public authority. Therefore no further examination on their part is needed.[6]

The tradition of having Christians participate in war became well established. The just war became the dominant ethic with respect to war. The alternative of pacifism was perceived to be a counsel of the Gospel and was not obligatory and, in fact, it often was perceived to be an inappropriate response when the state was in danger. Of course pacifism was expected of the clergy and of members of religious orders. Thus, while pacifism remained a modest option, the dominant and received tradition is that of sanctioning the participation of Christians in war.

# 2
# Survey of Roman Catholic Teachings on War and Peace

## The Early Church

As indicated in the previous chapter, the primary attention of the early Church was on its own spiritual development while awaiting the return of Jesus. Nonetheless as time passed and the world did not end nor appeared likely to do so, the Church became involved in the affairs of the world. The Church also grew numerically, and many of the new members were from a broader socio-economic background. A significant factor that slowed the Church's full assimilation into the Roman Empire was persecution based on perception that Christians threatened the stability of the empire because they would not participate in emperor worship and because of a feeling that this new religion could create political threats by providing an alternative ideological perspective which would disrupt the unity of the empire. Nonetheless, even in spite of serious persecutions, the Church continued to grow. When Constantine became the emperor early in the fourth century, Christianity became the official state religion of the Roman Empire and members of the Church, including the hierarchy, took an even more active role in the affairs of state.

Ambrose and Augustine have already been mentioned in terms of their development of justifications for a Christian's participation in war. On the other hand, both of these individuals continually made efforts to achieve peace. Ambrose, for example, demanded that Emperor Theodosius perform public penance for a massacre of the

17

inhabitants of Thessalonica. Augustine, too, made numerous appeals for peace and for clemency to help resolve the aftermath of the many wars to which he was a witness.

Pope Innocent I (402–417) served as a mediator between the Roman Empire and Alaric. This role was continued by Pope Leo I (440–461) in his appeal to Attila. Leo attempted to mediate again when Genseric led another Vandal invasion of the empire. Although not as successful as he was with Attila, Leo was able to restrain some of the excesses of the invasion. Gregory I (590–604) established some communication with the invading Lombards and helped maintain order within the developing empire. Unfortunately, for several centuries after Gregory, the Popes became embroiled in local politics and focused on their own political interests. Consequently, they were unable to serve as mediators.

In the year 910, the Abbey of Cluny was founded and began to help reform the religious and civil life of Europe. The abbot of Cluny was responsible for helping to initiate the Peace of God, the major intent of which was to exempt certain classes of persons from the operations of war and to mark off a sphere of peace. Basically non-combatants, defenseless people, and members of the clergy were not allowed to be attacked.

The movement was succeeded, in the eleventh century, by the Truce of God which served as a check on war by restricting the times when war could be fought. One truce prohibited fighting from Wednesday vespers to sunrise on Monday. Other truces prohibited fighting during liturgical seasons: from the beginning of Advent to the octave of the Epiphany, from the beginning of Easter to its octave, and from the first of the Rogation days to the octave of Pentecost. While not eliminating war or reducing the amount of violence that occurred during a war, both the Peace of God and the Truce of God, when strictly enforced, did at least restrict the time when fighting could occur and served as a check on the violence at that time. Pope Urban II (1088–1099), at the Council of Clermont, attempted to reintroduce the Truce of God and declare anathema those who broke it voluntarily. In the Council of Rheims in 1119, the Truce was reenacted and the Second Lateran Council put the final touches on its institutionalization, and the Third Lateran Council, in 1179, made the Truce universal law for the entire Church by making it part of canon law. This, of course, did not guarantee its observance, and eventually the Truce of God became part of the history of the Church rather than its active teaching.

Another very important limitation on war came through the preaching of the mendicant orders, especially the Franciscans. In addition to his own personal efforts to reduce violence in the Crusades, St. Francis also made it a part of the rule of the Third Order that members could not carry weapons on their person. This was a significant blow to warfare during feudal times and, in fact, helped reduce war qualitatively and quantitatively.

### The Medieval Church

During the Middle Ages, the Church achieved a major point of development. Part of this was due to the growing unity of the Roman Empire and part was due to the presence of a number of gifted individuals such as the founders of the mendicant orders, several brilliant theologians such as Aquinas and Bonaventure, and an extremely gifted Pope, Innocent III. During this time the theory of the just war reached a point of major synthesis in the systematic development of Catholic theology. As already mentioned, Aquinas put into a more structured form the insights of Ambrose and Augustine. Aquinas was followed in his reflections on war by the theologians Vitoria and Suarez.

Vitoria, in his *De Jure Belli,* summarizes the three rules of war as follows:

First Canon: Assuming that a prince has authority to make war, he should first of all not go seeking occasions and causes of war, but should, if possible, live in peace with all men as St. Paul enjoins on us.

Second Canon: When war for a just cause has broken out it must not be waged so as to ruin the people to whom it is directed, but only so as to obtain one's rights and the defense of one's country and in order that from that war peace and security may in time result.

Third Canon: When victory has been won and victory
should be utilized with moderation and Christian humility,
and the victor ought to deem that he is sitting as judge between two states, the one which has been wronged and the
one which has done the wrong, so that it will be as judge
and not as accuser that he will deliver the judgment whereby the injured state can obtain satisfaction, and this, so far
as possible, should involve the offending state in the least
degree of calamity and misfortune, the offending individuals being chastised within lawful limits.[7]

The focus here is on the more significant obligation to preserve
the peace and fight only when necessary. On the other hand, Vitoria recognizes that war may break out and he constructs his summary in terms of the obligations governing a warring country, especially
with respects to the limits of what it can do after one country has
won.

Suarez also presents a summary of his just war theory:

In order that war may be justly waged, certain conditions
are to be observed and these may be brought under three
heads. First it must be waged by a legitimate power. Second, its cause must be just and right. Third, just methods
should be used, that is, equity in the beginning of the war
and the prosecution of it and in victory: all these are evident from the following sections. The reason of the general
conclusion is that although war, in itself, is not an evil, yet
on account of the many ills which it brings in its train, it is
to be numbered among those undertakings which are often
wrongly done. And thus it needs many circumstances to
make it honest.[8]

The major way in which this summary differs from the previous
one is that it focuses on the means by which war is conducted. That
is, it focuses primarily on the *jus in bello.* Of special importance is
Suarez's notation that even though war is not evil, because of the
way it can be conducted it may become evil, and thus one needs to

attend, in particular, to the circumstances in which it is conducted to make it just.

The conduct of the Christians during the Crusades frequently gave the lie to the moral teaching in the limits of war and violence. Zeal for the faith and hatred of the Arabs combined to blind most Christians so that they could not restrain their own conduct, much less evaluate it. During and after the Protestant Reformation, there were many hideous wars of religion in which Christians fought each other to establish the purity of their doctrine. This was followed, primarily in Spain, by the Inquisition which caused much suffering to many innocent people, but was again justified by the need for purity of religion. Although during this time period the Popes served as mediators in various wars, especially between France and England as well as for many other nations, it is the case that the Church both participated in and encouraged much of the violence of that time. The picture of the Church during the Middle Ages is not all negative with respect to its participation in war and other forms of institutionalized violence; nonetheless the Church participated more and more in the affairs of state and at times became identified exclusively with particular rulers as they attempted to achieve their political ends, through both statecraft and war.

**The Modern Church**

Many Popes in the modern age continued the role of mediator, especially during the many wars that occurred in Europe.[9] Pius IX attempted to mediate the Franco-German war but neither side seemed to wish to settle the dispute. In the aftermath of the war, the Catholic Church lost its territory in Italy known as the Papal States. While causing many problems especially in the relations between the Catholic Church and Italy, nonetheless the loss of territorial sovereignty allowed future Popes to be perceived as neutrals since they no longer had extensive territorial holdings to worry about.

Leo XIII was sought as a mediator in various disputes by Germany, Spain, England, Portugal, and Belgium. In his 1881 encyclical letter, *Diuturnum Illud,* Leo XIII suggested that the Pope could serve as a mediator for international disputes. In 1889, he condemned the use of aggressive wars to settle national differences. He encouraged several peace conferences and, in 1900, performed a symbolic example of disarmament by melting down old swords and selling them as scrap iron.

Pius X became Pope as an arms race was beginning in Europe and hostility between nations was developing. In 1905, Pius X condemned strident nationalism and a policy of might makes right. In spite of his efforts, though, Pius X was not able to persuade the nations of Europe to refrain from fighting, and in 1914 war broke out.

Benedict XV continued the efforts of Pius X by appealing for peace among the nations. In his 1914 encyclical he proposed an armistice; in his Christmas message he attempted to arrange a truce, and in August 1917 he sent a note to various belligerents outlining definite proposals for peace. However, whether because of a perception of an improper political interference on the part of the Pope or because of religious prejudice, Benedict XV was not allowed to participate in bringing World War I to an end.

After Benedict's death, Pius XI continued his effort and made many significant contributions to the development and preservation of peace. Pius XI spoke out against the delusion of preserving peace through armaments, critiqued nationalism, both economic and political, and urged that peace education programs be developed by the hierarchy. His focus on the need for internationalism and a recognition of the unity of all people is summarized in the following quotation from his encyclical letter *Ubi Arcano Dei.*

> Love of country becomes merely an occasion, an added incentive to grave injustice, when true love of country is debased to the condition of an extreme nationalism, when we forget that all men are our brothers and members of the same great human family, and that other nations have an equal right with us both to life and to prosperity.[10]

Pope Pius XII succeeded Pius XI and experienced many problematic situations during his pontificate. These included, but were not limited to, World War II, the holocaust, and the development of nuclear weapons. Since Pius XII was also one of the more prolific Popes, it will not be possible to go into great detail on all of his statements on war and peace. However, it is important to present several significant statements of his to obtain an overview of his orientation.

Pope Pius XII continually placed before his various audiences the ideal of peace and the conditions necessary for peace as well as teaching the legitimate means to preserve peace. Wars, the Pope felt, were caused by a type of spiritual anemia as well as a non-observance of the laws of God and nature. Peace would come through a deepening of spirituality and a development of appropriate moral dispositions. Continually Pius XII rooted his version of peace in observing the needs of justice and charity.

With respect to the kind of wars that could be fought, Pius XII made two important statements. First, he continued the tradition of prohibiting wars of aggression. In his 1944 Christmas message, he indicated that the immorality of the war of aggression has become more evident than before. And in his 1948 Christmas message, he said:

> Every war of aggression against these goods which the Divine plan for peace obliges men unconditionally to respect and guarantee and accordingly to protect and defend is a sin, a crime, an outrage against the majesty of God, the Creator and Ordainer of the world.

Second, he continued to teach the legitimacy of a war of self-defense and underscored the right, and even necessity, of a country to defend itself. This dimension of his teaching was reiterated several times during his pontificate.

For example, in his 1940 Christmas message, in discussing the premises for a new world order, Pius said: "This conception [that might can create right] does not exclude the desire for the honorable improvement of conditions or the right to defend oneself if peaceable life has been attacked, or to repair the damage sustained thereby."[12]

In his 1948 Christmas message, Pius XII said:

> A person threatened with an unjust aggression, or already its victim, may not remain passively indifferent, if one would think and act as befits Christians. All the more does the solidarity of the family of nations forbid others to be-

have as mere spectators, in an attitude of apathetic neutrality. Who will ever measure the harm already caused in the past by such indifference to war of aggression, which was quite alien to the Christian instinct?[13]

Later on in that same message, he said:

One thing, however, is certain: the commandment of peace is a matter of Divine Law. Its purpose is the protection of goods of humanity, inasmuch as they are gifts of the Creator. Among these goods are those of such importance for society that it is perfectly lawful to defend them against unjust aggression. Their defense is even an obligation for the nations, as a whole, who have a duty not to abandon a nation that is attacked.[14]

The necessity of the ethical correctness of a war of defense was further recognized in an address on international medical law on October 19, 1953 in which Pius XII said: "Every war should be punished on the international plane unless it be demanded by the absolute necessity of self-defense against a very grave injustice affecting the whole community which cannot be prevented by other means."[15]

The right to self-defense also included the right to use atomic weapons. In a rather strained statement, Pius said in his 1956 Christmas message:

The actual situation, which has no equivalent in the past, ought nevertheless to be clear to everyone. There is no further room for doubt about the purposes and message that lie behind tanks when they clash resoundingly across frontiers to distribute death and to force civilized peoples to a form of life that they distinctly abhor. When all the possible stages of negotiations and mediation are bypassed, and when the threat is made to use atomic arms to obtain concrete demands, whether these are justified or not, it becomes clear that, in present circumstances, there may come into existence in a nation a situation in which all hope of avoiding war becomes vain. In this situation, war of efficacious self-defense against unjust attacks, which is undertaken with hope of success, cannot be considered illicit.[16]

Another dimension of Pius XII's teaching that is of significance has to do with a statement of conscientious objection. In his 1956 Christmas message, he also said:

> If, therefore, a body representative of the people and the government—both having been chosen by free elections— in the moment of extreme danger, decides, by legitimate instruments of internal and external policy, on defensive precautions, and carries out the plans which they consider necessary, it does not act immorally. Therefore, a Catholic citizen cannot invoke his own conscience in order to refuse to serve and fulfill those duties the law imposes. On this matter we feel that we are in perfect harmony with our predecessors, Leo XIII and Benedict XV, who never denied that obligation, but lamented the headlong armaments race and the moral dangers accompanying barracks life and urged, as we do likewise, general disarmament as an effective remedy.[17]

This statement has two dimensions: as stated previously, a state has the right to declare war—even nuclear war—to defend itself; once that has been done appropriately by the government, individuals may not invoke their conscience to exempt themselves from service to the country in fighting the war. The importance of this teaching is to remove the responsibility for such decision making from the individual and to place it on the shoulders of the state. Then, once the state has decided, the individual must conform to the authority of the state. Given the clarity of this statement and Pius' own valuing of ecclesiastical authority, it is no wonder that many people felt that it was impossible for a Catholic to be a conscientious objector to war in general or, more specifically, when a country had legitimately declared a war of self-defense.

However, the context in which war was conducted and the continued development of new and more powerful atomic weapons created a situation which gave rise to other considerations and to the beginnings of a re-evaluation of the traditional teaching on war as well as the application of that teaching to the current situation.

## Contemporary Papal Teaching

### John XXIII

The encyclical *Pacem in Terris,* written in 1963, was the first major statement on peace to be issued by a Pope in many years. Pope John XXIII dealt with the problem of war and the solution of peace in the third section of this encyclical which deals with the relations between states. He makes two general points. First, truth and justice are the main norms by which the relations between states are to be regulated, and this regulation is to produce an atmosphere of active solidarity so that states can work together to promote the national and international common good—"the sum total of those conditions of social living whereby men are enabled to achieve their own integral perfection more fully and more easily." Second, Pope John argues that the arms race destroys truth and justice and, therefore, breaks down attempts to actualize solidarity among nations.

Pope John argued that the arms race violates justice because it channels intellectual and economic resources into the development of the weapons of destruction and, consequently inhibits economic and social progress. Pope John also argued that the ever-increasing number of weapons has the likelihood of setting off a war, even though this be accidental. He also suggested that the testing of nuclear weapons, an inherent part of the arms race, has the potential to jeopardize various kinds of life on the earth. In summary, the arms race deprives individuals and nations of the resources they need to develop their own common good and jeopardizes the well-being of people by increasing the likelihood of war and by harming the environment in which people live.

The more critical comment of Pope John, however, is directed toward nuclear war itself. He says: "Therefore, in an age such as ours which prides itself on its atomic energy, it is contrary to reason to hold that war is now a suitable way to restore rights which have been violated."[18] Even though this translation has frequently been questioned and others suggest that it should be very narrowly interpreted, nonetheless Pope John seriously challenges the moral viability of nuclear war. And that challenge was picked up by many individuals and sparked a re-evaluation of war in Roman Catholic theology. Perhaps that is Pope John's greatest legacy to us: that he encouraged the rethinking of the traditional ethic of war and that he was a prophet who shook us out of a lethargy which accepted nuclear war as a means of vindicating rights.

## Paul VI

Pope Paul VI, in his encyclical *Populorum Progressio,* written in 1967, also spoke to the problem of war and violence. The primary focus of this encyclical is on the social conditions necessary for achieving appropriate levels of development. Part of the problem addressed is the fact of social injustice and the means to overcome it. In general, Pope Paul VI's orientation was to achieve development through structural reform and the development of those social conditions which will enhance human dignity. He also recognized, however, the fact that injustice and dependency can make the recourse to violence to achieve one's goals a serious temptation, and in regard to this he stated:

> We know, however, that a revolutionary uprising—save where there is manifest, long-standing tyranny which would do great damage to fundamental personal rights and dangerous harm to the common good of the country—produces new injustices, throws more elements out of balance and brings on new disasters. A real evil should not be fought against at the cost of greater misery.[19]

Although not directly addressed to the problem of war these words do argue that recourse to violence typically does not resolve problems and, in fact, creates more problems than it solves. However, Pope Paul provided no critique for evaluating what many came to call a justified revolution or a justification for a war of national liberation. Although not necessarily applicable to the relationships between different sovereign nations, nonetheless the exception that Pope Paul presents stands in the tradition of the justified use of violence within the Roman Catholic moral tradition.

Pope Paul VI continued his critique of war through his statements on the arms race, disarmament, and development. Following very much in the line of Pope John XXIII, he linked peace with a reallocation of national resources to the poor and to the common good. For him, justice, which is the key to development, is the means to peace.

In his 1976 address on World Peace Day, Pope Paul VI also critiqued the arms race in the following terms.

What a loss in terms of education, culture, agriculture, health and civic life. True peace and life struggle on under an enormous and incalculable burden so that a peace based on the perpetual threat to life may be maintained and life may be defended by a constant threat to peace![20]

In a 1978 message to the United Nations, Pope Paul said:

Resource to arms is a scandalous thing. The thought of disarmament on the other hand awakens great hope. The scandal is due to the crying disproportion between the resources of money and mind that are put at the service of the dead and those that are devoted to the service of life. The hope is that, as military expenditures lessen, a substantial part of the immense resources they preempt today may be used for a vast project of development on a world scale.[21]

Paul VI's hope was that by eliminating the causes of injustice and by promoting an authentic human development among all nations and peoples of the world, various forms of international cooperation would occur that would decrease the enmity that exists between different nations and, consequently, peace would be achieved. We must always keep in mind Paul VI's impassioned plea at the United Nations: "No more war, war never again! Never one against the other."

*John Paul II*

Pope John Paul II, himself the victim of terrorist violence, has proven to be an outspoken advocate for peace. On a very practical level, he has at least helped facilitate a dialogue which has kept a semblance of political harmony and peace in his native Poland. He has also offered to serve as a mediator in various disputes and problematic areas existing between different nations. And while he has demanded that priests and religious do not directly intervene in political events, especially by holding public office, nonetheless he himself has provided an interesting example of how one might engage in political activity by leading the singing of nationalistic songs while visiting in Poland.

John Paul II has made two important statements on peace. The first comes from his encyclical letter *Redemptor Hominis:*

> These words become charged with even stronger warning when we think that, instead of bread and cultural aid, the new states and nations awakening to independent life are being offered, sometimes in abundance, modern weapons and means of destruction placed at the service of armed conflicts and wars that are not so much a requirement for defending their just rights and their sovereignty but rather a form of chauvinism, imperialism and neo-colonialism of one kind or another. We all know well that the areas of misery and hunger on our globe could have been made fertile in a short time if the gigantic investments for armaments at the service of war and destruction had been changed into investments for food at the service of life.
>
> For this reason the Church does not cease to implore each side of the two and to beg everybody in the name of God and in the name of man: do not kill! Do not prepare destruction and extermination for man! Think of your brothers and sisters who are suffering hunger and misery! Respect each one's dignity and freedom![22]

This quotation reflects a traditional emphasis in Catholic documents for the last twenty years: increased military budgets have tak-

en away money that could have been used for the development of
farmlands or the procuring of food and in this way have insured that
people will not be able to eat and have provided newer weapons with
means of destruction rather than means of survival. The Pope suggests that the priority should be relieving human hunger and suffering rather than preparing for the destruction of the human race.

When Pope John Paul II addressed the United Nations in October 1979, he said:

> The ancients said: "Si vis pacem, para bellum." But can
> our age really believe that the breathtaking spiral of arma-
> ments is at the service of world peace? In alleging the
> threat of a potential enemy, is it really not rather the inten-
> tion to keep for oneself a means of threat, in order to get
> the upper hand with the aid of one's own arsenal of de-
> struction? Here too it is the dimension of peace that tends
> to vanish in favor of ever a new possible form of imperial-
> ism.[23]

The point that the Pope makes here is that the arms race, rather
than being a form of national security, is actually a threat to the
peace of the world and is simply a means of being able to continually
threaten one's enemies. Also, in an important way, the Pope links the
arms race and imperialism, for those who have the power of ultimate
destruction may also be able to obtain the power to control the
world. Such elements, the Pope suggests, make peace impossible and
cause it to vanish. Perhaps one can paraphrase the ancient wisdom
by suggesting, especially in the light of the previous quotation from
his encyclical, that if we wish peace, we should prepare the earth so
that we can harvest its riches and relieve hunger and suffering.

## Contemporary Church Documents

### Vatican Council II

The convening of the Second Vatican Council provided the first
occasion in almost a century for the Church as a whole to reflect on

its situation in the modern world. Pope John XXIII wanted the Church to bring itself up to date, to address contemporary problems, and to take part in the discussion of the major questions of the day. For better or worse, one of the questions that the Council had to address was the question of war.

Probably the most widely quoted statement from Vatican II with respect to war is that one should approach the evaluation of war "with an entirely new attitude."[24] The primary reason for such a new attitude, indicated by the Council, is the development of weapons which "can inflict massive and indiscriminate destruction far exceeding the bounds of legitimate defense."[25] It is within this framework that the Council Fathers made the following pronouncement which, together with the condemnation of abortion, is the only condemnation to be found in the entire body of the Council document.

> With these truths in mind, this most holy synod makes its own the condemnations of total wars already pronounced by recent popes, and issues the following declaration: Any act of war aimed indiscriminately at the destruction of entire cities or extensive areas, along with their population, is a crime against God and man himself. It merits unequivocal and unhesitating condemnation.[26]

Together with this strong condemnation, however, the Council Fathers did not revoke the right of national self-defense. They said:

> Certainly, war has not been rooted out of human affairs. As long as the danger of war remains and there is no competent and sufficiently powerful authority at the international level, governments cannot be denied the right to legitimate defense once every means of peaceful settlement has been exhausted. Therefore, government authorities and others who share public responsibilities have an obligation to protect the welfare of the people entrusted to their care and to conduct such grave matters soberly.[27]

Together with this validation of the legitimacy of self-defense, the Council also made a positive statement about the role of those involved in the military: "Those who are pledged to the service as members of its armed forces should regard themselves as agents of security and freedom on behalf of their people. As long as they fulfill this role properly, they are making a genuine contribution to the establishment of peace."[28]

Even though the Council made these positive statements about the legitimacy of war as a means of self-defense when all other means have failed and gave a positive sanction to the role of individuals who are in the military, nonetheless it upheld the necessity to evaluate morally the waging of war.

> It is one thing to undertake military action for the just defense of the people, and something else again to seek the subjugation of other nations. Nor does the possession of war potential make every military or political use of it lawful. Neither does the mere fact that war has unhappily begun mean that all is fair between the warring parties.[29]

And remembering many of the atrocities that occurred specifically in World War II in Nazi Germany, but anticipating new atrocities—especially the increased use of torture by the military—the Council said the following:

> Contemplating this melancholy state of humanity, the Council wishes to recall first of all the permanent binding force of universal natural law and its all-embracing principles. Man's conscience itself gives an ever more emphatic voice to these principles. Therefore, actions which deliberately conflict with these same principles, as well as others commanding such actions, are criminal. Blind obedience cannot excuse those who yield to them. Among such must first be counted those actions designed for the methodological extermination of an entire people, nation, or ethnic minority. These actions must be vehemently condemned as horrendous crimes. The courage of those who openly and fearlessly resist such commands merits supreme commendation.[30]

But the most surprising aspect of the Council's deliberation is reflected in its teachings on pacifism and conscientious objection. In part, they represent a stark departure from the teaching of Pius XII, but on the other hand they reflect a culmination of a development of a new form of thought with regard to war and peace initiated by John XXIII and continued by Paul VI. The Council said:

> For this reason, all Christians are urgently summoned "to practice the truth in love" (Eph. 4:15) and to join with all true peacemakers in pleading for peace and bringing it about. Motivated by this same spirit, we cannot fail to praise those who renounce the use of violence in the vindication of their right and who resort to methods of defense which are otherwise available to weaker parties too, provided that this can be done without injury to the rights and duties of others or of the community itself.[31]

The Council then added:

> Moreover, it seems right that laws make human provisions for the case of those who for reasons of conscience refuse to bear arms, provided, however, that they accept some other form of service to the human community.[32]

This teaching represents a dramatic step forward in that for the first time an official Church teaching on an international level recognizes the right of conscientious objection and praise is given to those who would use the strategy of non-violence or perhaps adopt a pacifist lifestyle. The Council recognized that there are a plurality of opinions with respect to war and peace within the Catholic community, and it sanctioned a variety of ways of responding to this critical issue. On the one hand, the Council reaffirmed, in light of the lack of an international authority, the right of self-defense, but on the other hand it positively praised those who seek ways other than war to resolve international conflict. The Council also stated its deep concern about modern means of warfare and the extreme destruction they can bring about, and it also expressed extreme hesitation about the arms race as a means of insuring a lasting peace. Furthermore, following many other official teachings, it recognized that the arms race draws off money from other worthy social concerns and from the poor and, in fact, creates a trap from which humankind may not escape.

The Council provided no final resolution with respect to the question of war or peace, but more importantly it recognized that one needs to rethink the issue of war and peace with a new added truth in the light of the changed circumstances of modern warfare, and it also gave clear praise and sanction to the rights of those who choose to be conscientious objectors or pacifists.

### Report of the Holy See to the United Nations General Assembly

This very interesting document, presented by Msgr. Giovanni Cheli, permanent observer for the Holy See at the United Nations, while focusing on disarmament, also presents some extremely strong views about the means of conducting war. The document argues that the arms race is unjust because it amounts to a violation of rights by giving primacy to force, and then the stockpiling of weapons becomes an excuse for recourse to the increased exercise of naked power. It is also unjust because it is an act of theft that takes money that could be used for public funds and uses it for the manufacture and stockpiling of arms. The document argues that such a use of funds for arms while many unsatisfied vital needs exist, especially in developing countries, is basically an act of criminal agression. The document also asserts that the arms race is an absurdity because it is a means disproportionate to the end and, therefore, cannot guarantee security. The arms race does not increase security because there is already an overabundance of weapons, and added arms present only an overkill. The document states: "The arms race institutionalizes disorder and thus becomes a *perversion of peace*."[33]

The report sets out clearly a condemnation of the arms race— first, in the name of peace which the arms race does not secure, and, second, in the name of natural morality and the evangelical ideal. The document applies two principles here on which it bases this judgment. First, there is no longer a proportion between the harm caused and the values to be protected, and, therefore, it is better to suffer injustice then to defend oneself, or at least to defend oneself by means such as these. Second, when the use of weapons has for its principal use, not defense but aggression, it loses its reason for being, its justification, and its legitimacy. The document then concludes:

> In this kind of activity, we no longer have simply a cold war but an offensive action, *an unacceptable act of aggression and oppression.*[34]

## The American Church

### *Pastoral Letters*

#### (a) Human Life in Our Day

In this letter, issued in 1968, the American bishops continued the tradition, set out by Pius XII, of condemning without qualification wars of agression. They said, "Whatever case there may have seemed to exist in other times for wars fought for the domination of another nation, such a case can no longer be imagined given the circumstances of modern warfare, the heightened sense of mutuality and the increasingly available humane means to the realization of that mutuality."[35]

The bishops also endorsed the condemnation of wars fought without limitation, issued by Vatican Council II. In a concluding section, the American bishops developed a positive teaching on conscientious objection. In validating the individuals who are searching their conscience, especially with respect to the morality of participation in war, they said:

> As witnesses to a spiritual tradition which accepts enlightened conscience, even when honestly mistaken, as the immediate arbiter of moral decisions, we can only feel reassured by this evidence of individual responsibility and the decline of uncritical conformism to patterns some of which included strong moral elements, to be sure, but also included political, social, cultural and like controls not necessarily in conformity with the mind and heart of the Church.

If war is ever to be outlawed, and replaced by a more humane and enlightened institution to regulate conflicts among nations, institutions rooted in the notion of universal common good, it will be because the citizens of this and other nations have rejected the tendency of exaggerated nationalism and insisted on principles on non-violent political and civil action in both the domestic and international spheres.[36]

The American bishops went on to endorse the statements of Vatican II which praised those who renounced the use of violence to vindicate their rights and suggested, also in light of Vatican II, that provision be made for those who refuse to bear arms. But then, in a surprising move, they went further than the Council and followed the logic of the just war theory to its final conclusion. The bishops said:

The present laws of this country, however, provide only for those whose reasons of conscience are grounded in a total rejection of use of military force. This form of conscience objection deserves the legal protection made for it but we consider that the time has come to urge that similar considerations be given to those whose consciences are more personal and specific.[37]

We therefore recommend a modification of the Selective Service Act making it possible, although not easy, for so-called selective conscientious objectors to refuse—without fear of imprisonment or loss of citizenship—to serve in wars which they consider unjust or in branches of service (e.g., the strategic nuclear forces) which would subject them to actions contrary to deeply held moral convictions about indiscriminate killing. Some other form of service to the human community should be required of those so exempted.[38]

The option of selective objection is, of course, a corollary of the just war theory but many were surprised when the American bishops explicitly announced their acceptance of such an option and also suggested that provisions be made in law for this option. That is, of course, in direct contradiction to the teaching already mentioned of Pius XII that when a country has legitimately declared a war, no one can object to it. The current teaching of the American bishops represents a development in the teaching about war especially in light of the circumstance of contemporary nuclear warfare.

This letter also focused on one specific weapon: the neutron bomb. The bishops said:

> Nothing more dramatic would suggest the anti-life direction of technological warfare than the neutron bomb; one philosopher declares that the manner in which you will leave entire cities intact, but totally without life, makes it, perhaps, the symbol of our civilization. It would be perverse indeed if the Christian conscience were to be unconcerned or mute in the face of the multiple moral aspects of these warsome prospects.[39]

Of course, this dramatic statement seems to have been forgotten when discussions of the development and use of this weapon took place in the late 1970s and early 1980s. This particular weapon does have the advantage, however, of revealing our true priorities: property is more important than life.

### (b) To Live as Christ Jesus

This pastoral letter focused, in part, on the use of nuclear weapons. The important element in this teaching of the American bishops is the following statement.

> With respect to nuclear weapons, at least those with massive destructive capability, the first imperative is to prevent their use. As possessors of a vast nuclear arsenal, we must also be aware that not only is it wrong to attack civilian populations, but it is also wrong to threaten to attack them as part of a strategy of deterrence. We urge the continued development and implementation of policies which seek to bring these weapons more securely under control, progres-

sively reduce their presence in the world, and ultimately remove them entirely.[40]

This statement strikes directly at the heart of the deterrence theory by arguing that it is wrong to threaten to attack civilian populations or, in the terms of the just war theory, to attack innocent
non-combatants. It would have been interesting if the American
bishops had drawn out specific behavioral consequences for Catholics, especially those who are involved in some way in either the production or the potential use of such weapons.

## The United States Catholic Conference

The United States Catholic Conference is the administrative
arm of the National Conference of Catholic Bishops, and while it
does not speak with the same authority as the bishops of the country,
nonetheless it is responsible for putting together statements which reflect current Catholic teachings. Statements made by the USCC have
at least been reviewed by the bishops, if not directly sanctioned by
them.

A variety of statements have been made by the USCC either as
an organization or by individuals speaking on its behalf that are related to issues of war and peace. While some of these simply repeat
material that we have previously mentioned, other statements carry
this teaching a little bit further.

For example, an October 1969 statement on "Catholic Conscientious Objection" basically repeats the teaching found in the pastoral letter "On Human Life in Our Day." But in addition to this
wider promulgation of the teaching, the USCC also makes two recommendations: (1) that each diocese initiate or cooperate in providing draft information and counseling; (2) that Catholic organizations
which could qualify as alternative service agencies consider applying
for that status and support and provide meaningful employment for
the conscientious objector. The important thing about these recommendations is that they begin to put into practice on a diocesan level
a means of implementing this particular position on conscientious
objection. This position should also indicate the appropriateness of

the role of individual conscience in determining whether one is or is not a conscientious objector and provide official support for those individuals who choose the route of conscientious objection.

A 1978 statement entitled "The Gospel of Peace and the Danger of War" indicated that the primary moral imperative at the present time is that "the arms race must be stopped and the reduction of armaments must be achieved." Several objectives are then identified: the superpower arms race must be brought under control both quantitatively and qualitatively, the proliferation of nuclear weapons must be restrained, and restrictions must be placed on the rapid growth of conventional arms sales in the world. The document concludes with the following exhortation:

> To pursue peace in the political process requires courage; at times it means taking risks for peace. The Church in a competent and careful manner must encourage reasonable risks for peace. To risk requires a degree of faith, and faith, in turn, is based on the hope that comes from prayer. As the Church in this nation, we seek to be a moral voice placing restraints on war, a prophetic voice calling for peace, and a prayerful community which has the courage to work for peace.[41]

Also, on occasion, individuals will speak on behalf of the United States Catholic Conference, and two instances of this are extremely important for the discussion of the ethical debate on war and peace in the United States Catholic community. The first presentation is the testimony of Cardinal Krol of Philadelphia to the Senate Foreign Relations Committee in 1976 which was taking testimony on the SALT II Treaty. In this testimony, Cardinal Krol made several important statements with respect to Roman Catholic teaching on war and peace. While Cardinal Krol was speaking on behalf of the USCC, his brother bishops, and the Catholics of the nation, it is too much to expect that everyone would agree with everything that he said. What is important to keep in mind, however, is that Cardinal Krol is one of the more conservative cardinals of the country and many times has been perceived to be very much on the side of the status quo, both politically and socially.

Early in his testimony, Cardinal Krol said:

This role requires me to speak the truth plainly. The Catholic bishops of this country believe that too long have we Americans been preoccupied with preparations for war. Too long have we been guided by the false criterion of equivalence or superiority of armanents; too long have we allowed other nations to virtually dictate how much we should spend on stockpiling weapons of destruction. Is it not time that we concentrate our efforts on peace rather than war? Is it not time that we take that first step toward peace; gradual, bilateral, negotiated disarmament?[42]

In this statement Cardinal Krol is challenging some of the priorities of our country, especially from the defense point of view. He suggests that for a long time we have been looking in the wrong direction and have been guided by false criteria for security.

Another important statement in his testimony is the following:

In a nuclear age, the moral sanctions against war have taken on a qualitatively new character. From Pius XII to John Paul II, the moral argument is clear: the nuclear arms race is to be unreservedly condemned and the political process of arms control and disarmament is to be supported by the Christian community.[43]

This is an extremely strong statement because it says that the nuclear arms race is to be condemned. One could assume that certain behavioral implications would flow from the fact that the nuclear arms race is condemned. For example, does this condemnation mean that individuals may no longer participate in building nuclear weapons? Does it mean that individuals may not serve in a branch of the armed services which would deliver such a weapon to another country? Does it mean that military chaplains should teach the Catholic soldiers under their jurisdiction that they may no longer participate in a form of military service related to nuclear weapons and that they should disobey the commands of their superiors? These are very hard questions but they have a very practical bearing on the statement made by Cardinal Krol.

Cardinal Krol also made one other lengthy statement that deserves quotation because of the seriousness of the implications that flow from it:

> The moral paradox of deterrence is that its purpose is to prevent the use of nuclear weapons, but it does so by an expressed threat to attack the civilian population of one's adversary. Such a threat runs directly counter to the central moral affirmation of the Christian teaching on war: that innocent lives are not open to direct attack. The complexity of that moral dilemma is reflected in the statement on deterrence of the American bishops in 1976: With respect to nuclear weapons, at least those with massive destructive capability, the first imperative is to prevent their use. As possessors of a vast nuclear arsenal, we must also be aware that not only is it wrong to attack civilian population but it is also wrong to threaten to attack them as part of a strategy of deterrence. We urge the continued development and implementation of policies which seek to bring these weapons more securely under control, progressively reduce their presence in the world, and ultimately remove them entirely (*To Live in Christ Jesus,* 1976).

The moral judgment of this statement is that not only the *use* of nuclear weapons but also the *declared intent* to use them in our deterrence policy is wrong. This explains the Catholic dissatisfaction with nuclear deterrence and the urgency of the Catholic demand that the nuclear arms race be reversed. It is of the utmost importance that negotiations proceed to meaningful and continued reductions in nuclear stockpiles, and eventually to the phasing out altogether of nuclear deterrence and the threat of mutually assured destruction.

As long as there is hope of this occurring, Catholic moral teaching is willing, while negotiations proceed, to tolerate the possession of nuclear weapons for deterrence as the lesser of two evils. If that hope were to disappear, the moral attitude of the Catholic Church would almost certainly have to shift to one of uncompromising condemnation of both use *and* possession of such weapons.[44]

This lengthy quotation contains a very succinct and accurate summary of Roman Catholic teaching on deterrence policy. The critical comment, however, is in the last paragraph, and the basic issue is to determine whether at the present time the modest hope that Cardinal Krol holds out is in fact true or not. One can certainly make an argument that the breaking off of the SALT II talks, the dramatic increase in our military budget, and the aggressive, hard line being taken toward many nations indicates that this hope may be disappearing. One also needs to be concerned about the increased discussions having to do with the possibility of winning a nuclear war. Such statements were made during the presidential campaign of George Bush, and they have been continued during the Reagan administration. However, Cardinal Krol presents an interesting test which must be applied to our current situation, and moral conclusions must be drawn from that.

Another individual who has given testimony on behalf of the United States Catholic Conference is Reverend Bryan Hehir, who is the Associate Secretary for International Justice and Peace. Again, while not everyone would agree with Father Hehir's testimony to the House Committee on Armed Services presented in March 1980, nonetheless it is important as a statement which reflects at least some degree of consensus with the USCC and, therefore, is reflective of at least the feeling, if not the thought, of the USCC. In this testimony, Father Hehir makes one important statement which articulates his perception of the state of the debate over war and peace in current Catholic theology. While we will be examining Father Hehir's own moral argument later in this book, it is important to put this quotation forward as his summary, on behalf of the USCC, of the state of the debate.

While it would be too much to conclude that Catholicism has adopted an in-principle position of pacifism as its sole response to modern war, it is possible to see that the nuclear age, and its attendant awesome danger, has moved Catholic moral teaching to affirm only a quite narrow justification of resort to arms. The shift of perspective in turn shapes the following principles which are at the heart of contemporary Catholic teaching on modern warfare:

1. Condemnation of the arms race as "an utterly treacherous trap for humanity" and "a danger and injustice, a theft from the poor and a folly." Correlatively, the Church has continually supported efforts of disarmament which would proceed "at an equal pace according to agreement and backed up by authentic and workable safeguards."

2. Condemnation of total war and the use of weapons which "can inflict immense and indiscriminate havoc that goes far beyond bounds of legitimate defense."

3. Support for the positions of conscientious objection and selective conscientious objection as means by which individuals can fulfill their duty to scrutinize whether specific forms of warfare are legitimate and justifiable.

4. Recognition of the right of the state "to legitimate defense once every means of peaceful settlement has been exhausted." The meaning of legitimate defense, however, is shaped by the previous three principles.[45]

The important thing about this statement, in addition to the concise articulation of the current Catholic teaching, is its recognition and affirmation that there has been a shift in the teaching on war in the Catholic theology that has been sanctioned at the highest official levels of Catholicism and has received support from many moral theologians as well as many other interested Catholic lay people. The basis for this shift undoubtedly has been the status of contemporary warfare, especially with respect to nuclear weapons. Another dimension of this shift of analysis has come from the arms race and the devoting of more and more time, energy, and money to the creation of weapons which, although designated as defensive, have the potential to destroy the entire world. And again, while not drawing any specific conclusion with reference to a particular situation, nonetheless the testimony provided by Father Hehir provides a framework for the analysis of many situations.

**Summary**

There are several important conclusions that follow from this survey of Roman Catholic teaching on war and peace.

1. There is a right of nations to defend themselves through force if all other means have failed to resolve the dispute. This right to defend oneself exists primarily because there is no international agency with sufficient power to serve as both a mediator of dispute and as a guarantee of the enforcement of treaties.

2. However, there has been a major shift in how war is perceived. It is the teaching of the Catholic Church at the present time that only a defensive war can be justified. That is, the right to defend oneself, mentioned above, can be exercised only when one is defending rights that have been violated. Total war and wars which seek to punish a neighboring country, for example, or wars which seek to expand one's boundaries are prohibited. Only a defensive war can be justified according to current Catholic teaching.

3. Contrary to the teaching of Pius XII, the Catholic Church now recognizes, at the highest levels, the right of an individual Catholic citizen to be either a complete conscientious objector or, more interestingly, to be a selective conscientious objector. The Catholic position on selective conscientious objection is one logical conclusion from the traditional use of just war categories to evaluate the morality of war. What is interesting about the acceptance of this possibility within the Roman Catholic tradition is that such a position is politically dangerous and illegal. The American Catholic Church, in particular, has gone on record as recommending that legal provisions be made for those who wish to assume this particular posture during a particular war.

4. Another important conclusion of current Catholic teaching on war has to do with the condemnation of the arms race. The arms race is seen as a waste of money because it puts one's hopes for security in a false and unsafe place and also as basically a form of theft in that money that could be spent for more important social goods is diverted toward destruction. This teaching reaches back to the views of Pius XII and has continued through the teachings of John Paul II.

5. Current Roman Catholic teaching also recognizes that there are grave moral difficulties with the development of nuclear weapons and the conducting of war using nuclear weapons. Part of the difficulties have to do with the strategy of deterrence which threatens to destroy civilian populations as well as the possible use of nuclear weapons which would destroy a disproportionate number of innocent people but which also have the potential to destroy the entire world. Nuclear weapons have been the major factor in initiating a reevaluation of the Roman Catholic Church's teaching on war. They present unique problems in that they threaten the destruction of the entire world, but they also have caused individuals to live in constant terror, and the cost of their production has been responsible for diverting money from other social projects.

What remains now for the Roman Catholic Church to do is to work through the process of determining what, if any, behavioral implications for the members of the Church will flow from these teachings. The drawing of specific conclusions from these general principles will be extremely problematic and will cause a great deal of dissension. Nonetheless, it can reasonably be argued that the task of the Church as a moral teacher is to draw conclusions that offer specific guidance to its members. This moral direction must extend to individuals who work in defense-related projects as well as to members of the armed services, including the chaplains. Also the Catholic Church must begin to think through what it means for the ordinary citizen to at least indirectly support nuclear warfare by the paying of taxes. One bishop recently recommended that Catholics withhold a portion of their income tax as a protest against the spending of that money on weapons of destruction. Such a recommendation is extremely problematic, not only because it is illegal, but also because it suggests that individuals have a significant responsibility in determining the political direction of their nation and that such a determination can be exercised in a very significant way: through the withholding of financial support for government projects. Such a position is not an argument against the paying of taxes but an argument supporting the position that Catholics may not cooperate in the doing of evil.

The days ahead are going to be extremely difficult for Roman Catholics with respect to the problem of war and peace. It is imperative at the present time that the Catholic Church provide appropriate guidance for the conducting of the debate on war and peace and also engage in the search for practical direction for how its members should conduct themselves in these critical and dangerous times.

# 3
# American Theological Reflection on War and Peace

Many American Catholic theologians have examined the morality of war. Such was the case especially in the 1950s when the pressure of the cold war made it appear likely that an actual war was a possibility. This discussion was also stimulated by the continued developments in nuclear weaponry, especially the transition from an atomic to a hydrogen bomb and in new modes of delivery. Most of the theological analysis in the 1950s and early 1960s was in the context of papal teachings and the cold war. As the Church began to change and develop, especially after Vatican Council II, there was also a shift in the moral analysis of the problem of war. This transition came about dramatically with the encyclical letter *Peace on Earth* of John XXIII. His intiatives on peace and his analysis of nuclear war spurred a whole new development in the moral analysis of war. One significant dimension was the shift from focusing only on the morality of war to the developing of a perspective focusing on peace and promoting peace. While this perspective was certainly not lacking in the earlier teaching, nonetheless I would describe the shift in the following way. The traditional orientation had seen peace as the conclusion of the just war teaching. The new orientation suggests that peace is the point of departure and the context in which the morality of war might be analyzed. Thus, one major element in the new orientation is the point of departure and the consequent development of a new context for analysis.

In this section of the book I will summarize several of the teachings of major Catholic theologians with respect to the morality of war. This survey will provide an orientation to both the content of the analysis as well as how that analysis has changed over the past years.

### John Ford, S.J.

John Ford's analysis of the morality of war and of practices within the conducting of war began with an acceptance of the possibility of war's being moral and its being conducted in a moral fashion. In a significant article entitled "The Morality of Obliteration Bombing," he states his position as follows:

> I do not intend to discuss here the question: Can any modern war be morally justified? The overwhelming majority of Catholic theologians would answer, I am sure, that there can be a justifiable modern war. And the practically unanimous voice of American Catholicism, including that of the hierarchy, assures us that we are fighting a just war at present. I accept that position.[46]

In his analysis of the morality of war and its practices, Ford distinguishes between what a confessor ought to do practically and what general moral principles ought to be and imply with respect to the moral evaluation of war. In determining confessional practice, Ford places emphasis on the conscience of the individual, especially given the fact that there may not be a clear Church teaching or clear moral consensus on a particular act or situation. For example, in 1941, Ford said that if the infallible Church has not spoken and will not speak on the justice of a given war and when Catholic hierarchies of opposing enemy nations speak on it and give opposite answers, and when moral theologians are still forming their opinions, "the very least we can say is that, as far as confessional practice is concerned, the sincere conscientious objector is entitled to the freedom of his conscience. The fact that he is Catholic does not make it wrong for him to be a conscientious objector, too."[47]

Ford continues this line by saying:

The impression made upon the present writer by reading
the foregoing literature (and much more like it) is that the
application of our moral principles to the modern world
leaves so much to be desired that we are not in a position to
impose obligations on the consciences of the individual,
whether he be a soldier with a bayonet or a conscientious
objector, *except in the cases where violation of natural law is
clear.*[48]

And again in an article before the strategy and tactics of World
War II were fully in place, Ford suggested that it seemed utterly in-
human to allow the bombing of civilians from the air. But then he
went on to say, "That problem remains to be answered; and, as we
said last year, in the meantime pilots and bombardiers may continue
to obey the orders of their superior officers, except in cases where it
is *certain* that an unjustifiable act on the innocent is being made."[49]

The problem of bombing, and, in particular, obliteration bombing, led Ford, in 1944, to focus on that particular problem in a
lengthy article in *Theological Studies.* While this article focuses explicitly on the problem of the morality of obliteration bombing, it is
also interesting in terms of his argument about the morality of the
conduct of war and how one constructs a moral argument.

Again, Ford proposes a twofold analysis: confessional practice
and a moral evaluation. With respect to the confessional, Ford again
argues that it is quite appropriate for a confessor to give absolution
to a bombardier who feels forced to carry out orders to take part in
obliteration bombing unless, of course, the penitent is convinced of
the immorality of the practice. The reasons for this are: the problem
is a comparatively new one, there may not be specific norms laid
down by ecclesiastical authorities, there is a well-established rule
based on the presumption which favors the following of commands
by the civil authorities, and, as stated earlier, Ford feels that application of moral principles to war leaves so much to be desired that we
should not impose obligations on the conscience of individuals unless
there is a certain violation of natural law. Having thus dealt with the

practical problem of how to handle individuals who confess participation in such bombing, Ford now develops his analysis which has
convinced him of the immorality of the practice of obliteration
bombing.

Ford defines obliteration bombing in the following way:

> Obliteration bombing is the strategic bombing, by means of
> incendiaries and explosives, of industrial centers of popula-
> tion in which the target to be wiped out is not a definite
> factory, bridge, or similar object, but a large area of a
> whole city, comprising one-third to two-thirds of its whole
> built-up area, and including by design the residential dis-
> tricts of working men and their families.[50]

Ford uses two traditional principles of the just war theory to argue against this practice: the immunity of non-combatants in warfare
and the violation of the principle of double effect.

Ford recognizes that, given the context of modern war, it can be
difficult to distinguish combatants from non-combatants. Nonetheless, he argues that such a distinction is valid and therefore that the
traditional principle of the innocence of non-combatants and the im-
permissibility to kill them still holds. He basically argues that even
though it may be difficult to draw the line, the fact of that difficulty
does not obliterate the line between innocence and guilt. Even
though there might be some uncertainty in the application of principles, that does not argue that the principles are, in fact, inapplicable.
Finally, in a very incisive comment, Ford identifies what I think is
the real problem. He says: "Is it not evident that the most radical
and significant change of all in modern warfare is not the increased
cooperation of civilians behind the lines of the armed forces, but the
enormously increased power of the armed forces to reach behind the
lines and attack civilians indiscriminately, whether they are thus cooperating or not?"[51] Thus, the real problem, in Ford's opinion, is not
the obliteration of the distinction between combatants or non-combatants or even a difficulty in drawing the distinction, but rather the
increased capacity to bomb cities randomly. Ford also develops an
empirical argument, based on population studies, that a large number of categories of working people cannot be construed in such a

way as to switch their category from non-combatants to combatants. Ford recognizes that many working people will, in fact, be indirectly or in some other fashion aiding the war cause. To expect anything else is simply impossible. Yet, Ford is quite content to argue that the fact of some indirect cooperation does not constitute a moral sanctioning to change the status of a person from non-combatant to combatant.

The other position that Ford uses to condemn obliteration bombing is that of the double effect which some individuals had used to try to justify it. His argument consists in a counterargument showing that the principle should not be applied in this particular situation. First, he looks at the question of intent and asks: "Is it possible to employ this procedure without directly intending the damage to innocent civilians and their property"[52]

Focusing primarily on civilians, Ford answers this question by saying:

> Looking at obliteration bombing as it actually takes place, can we say that the maiming and death of hundreds of thousands of innocent persons, which is its immediate result, is not directly intended, but merely permitted? Is it possible psychologically and honestly for the leaders who have developed and ordered the employment of this strategy to say that they do not intend any harm to innocent civilians?[53]

This answer leads Ford to conclude that it is impossible to engage in obliteration bombing without directly intending the destruction of, and harm to, innocent civilians. This orientation is strengthened by his quoting of various British and American documents which argue that the purpose of obliteration bombing is to undermine the morale of the Germans and to bring terror and devastation to the enemy nation. Ford argues that it is impossible to make civilian terrorization or the undermining of civilian morale an object of bombing without having a direct intent to injure and kill civilians. He says, "If one intends the end, terror, one cannot escape intending the principal means of obtaining that end, namely, the injury and death of civilians."[54]

Ford's other argument against the use of the double effect principle focuses on proportionality, and his basic point is that obliteration bombing violates proportionality because the alleged proportionate causes which justify the bombing are "speculative, future, and problematical, while the evil effect is definite, widespread, certain, and immediate."[55] This summarizes Ford's perception that the justification of obliteration bombing based on the fact that it will help win the war, that it will shorten the war, that it will save soldiers' lives, and that it will enable the Allies to liberate Europe and feed the starving people sooner is simply a rationalization of military strategy that serves as a pretext for destroying civilian populations so that the war can be won. Again, what Ford appropriately focuses on here are not individual acts of bombing, but the *strategy* of obliteration as such. And it is this accepted strategy that Ford sees as leading to disproportionate effects that cannot be justified by various ends.

Ford concludes his analysis by saying:

> Obliteration bombing, as defined, is an immoral attack on the rights of the innocent. It includes a direct intent to do them injury. Even if this were not true, it would still be immoral, because no proportionate cause could justify the evil done; and to make it legitimate would soon lead the world to the immoral barbarity of total war. The voice of the Pope and the fundamental laws of the charity of Christ confirm this condemnation.[56]

The interesting dimension of Ford's orientation is that while on the one hand he accepts the possibility of a war's being just and accepts the validity of the principles of the just war and other moral principles for analyzing that, he is quite willing to engage in the process of applying these principles to specific tactics used in the war and to draw appropriate moral conclusions. The other interesting dimension of Ford's analysis is his careful distinction between the conscience of an individual who is participating in the war and the moral evaluation of the policy as a whole. While relying in part on a methodology that looks to ecclesiastical authority for ultimate validation of an argument, nonetheless he is quite willing to formulate an argument that could lead the ecclesiastical authorities to make a moral judgment on a certain policy which would then be binding on all individuals. While Ford recognizes that certain practices can get utterly out of hand and lead to the total immorality of a particular war or the immorality of the way in which the war is conducted, nonetheless he accepts the idea that war can be a moral enterprise and focuses his moral analysis on the practices of war.

### Gerald Kelly, S.J.

Gerald Kelly continued the tradition of analyzing the problems of modern war, especially modern war conducted with atomic weapons, within a framework of the just war theory and the principle of double effect. In the comments that he has made on the problem of war, he began the process of thinking through the morality of atomic warfare. What is also interesting about Kelly's analysis, though not surprising in the light of the context of the cold war in which he developed it, is the role of war with respect to its preserving the rights of Christian civilization. In a rather interesting analysis, part of which is directed to a commentary on other opinions proposed by moral theologians, he states quite clearly several presuppositions which lead him to his conclusion on the legitimacy of the use of atomic weapons.

> All of us would undoubtedly agree that atomic weapons *should* be outlawed. Yet, in the supposition of the conflict between theistic, peace-seeking nations and atheistic, aggressive forces, such a compact is hardly possible. The atheist would choose his own weapon. Granted this supposition, I agree with Father Connell when he says that the use of the hydrogen bomb by the defensive nations *can be* justified. I also agree that when such a weapon is directed toward a military target, the damage to civilians can be explained as indirect, even though it be terribly devastating. Finally, I think that Father McCarthy is wrong in saying that there can be no proportionate reason for permitting this devastation; for, in a supposition I am making (which is certainly not unrealistic), there is a question of preserving the lives, as well as the religious and civic liberty, of more

than half the world. I think that this is a sufficient compensating reason for almost any amount of damage indirectly inflicted on the citizens of the atheistic/communistic lesser nations.

In expressing this opinion, I am not condoning unnecessary damage. We can fervently (or perhaps vainly) hope that a future war will not involve the unnecessary damage that characterized the last war. But, granted that the objectives are military targets, and granted the necessity of eliminating them in order to resist atheistic aggression, I am of the opinion that the concommitant civilian devastation can be justified. I would apply this opinion either to the use of a single H-bomb on the target of supreme importance or to the use of A-bombs on a number of less important military targets.[57]

What I think is important in this moral analysis is the ideological context in which it occurs. For example, I would wonder whether the same argument would take place if the aggressor nation was a Christian nation. It is unclear what the relevant criterion is here. Is it the fact that the country is atheistic that justifies bombing it, or is it the fact that it is atheistic and aggressive, or is it the fact that it is merely aggressive?

Kelly does not abandon the distinction between combatants and non-combatants, nor does he accept the concept of total war. What he does do, though, is allow a wider range of personal and property destruction than Ford seemed to be comfortable with. He bases this on the difficulty of distinguishing precisely between non-military and military targets and between combatants and non-combatants. Even though the targets should be military, the use of atomic weapons in a war for the survival of our civilization, he argues, can be justified even though this means a wide destruction of civilian lives.

Kelly also makes a brief, but interesting, comment on what has come to be called the morality of a first strike with nuclear weapons:

I also agree with Father Walsh that, once the United States was certain of an imminent attack by an aggressor with an atomic bomb, our government would have no obligation to await the attack before using atomic bombs on the military targets of the aggressor nation. In fact, I should think that there would be an obligation not to await such an attack.[58]

Again, the interesting feature of Kelly's argumentation is the continued acceptance of the categories of the just war with respect to nuclear warfare and the continued extension of traditional moral principles into the analysis of modern warfare. The interesting difference between Kelly's analysis and Ford's analysis is that of the intrusion of the explicit ideological context in which the argument is cast. Ford, for example, was quite willing to argue that the United States' policy of obliteration bombing was quite immoral. Kelly, on the other hand, sees the role of the United States as the preserver of Christian civilization and argues, therefore, that almost any amount of destruction would justify the survival of the free world. What I think we can learn from this is the necessity of being alert to how a moral argument can be shaped or controlled, wittingly or unwittingly, by an ideological perspective.

### John Courtney Murray, S.J.

Among the many significant contributions that Murray made to theology and American theology in particular was his continued reliance on and development of the natural law as a means for enhancing and resolving significant issues of our time. Murray was convinced that reason could work its way through the tangles of social difficulties and international conflicts and lead people to valid ideas on which all could agree and to which all could assent. In Murray's discussion of war, he provided us with three important dimensions: a summary statement of the just war theory in the late 1950s, a summary statement of the functions of a just war theory, and a statement on the role of conscience in applying the categories of the just war theories, especially with relation to selective conscientious objection.

In providing his summary of the just war theory, Murray follows quite closely the thought of Pius XII, but he also serves as a moral theologian by summarizing and interpreting that thought. The first general principle Murray affirms is that all wars of aggression, whether just or unjust, are morally proscribed. This principle states that there can be no war even to redress the violation of a nation's legal rights. Murray argues, in support of the Pope's orientation, that the use of force cannot be now a moral means for the redress of violated legal rights. No state may now take the cause of justice into its own hands: "Whatever the grievance of the state may be, and however objectionable it may find the status quo, warfare undertaken on the solemn decision of the national state is an immoral means for settling the grievance and for altering existing conditions."[59]

There are two basic reasons for this principle. First, the increased violence of war in the present condition disqualifies it as an apt and proportionate means for resolving international conflicts and even resolving unjust grievances. Second, the continued right of war as an attribute of national sovereignty would block the development of an international community with juridical power.

The second general principle is that a defensive war to repress injustice is morally admissible both in principle and in fact. Under this principle, Murray states four qualifications. First, the war must be imposed on a nation by an obvious and extremely grave injustice. Second, it must be, in fact, the last resort of the nation. Third, there must be a twofold proportionality. (1) "Consideration must be given to the proportion between the damage suffered in consequence of the perpetration of a grave injustice, and the damages that would be let loose by a war to repress the injustice." (2) "Pius XII requires another estimate of another proportion, between the evils unleashed by war and what he calls 'the solid probability of success' in the forceful repression of unjust action."[60] Fourth, a limitation must be placed on the use of force. In part, this principle relates to the kinds of weapons used, especially if they would utterly destroy all human life within their radius of action, but it also maintains the distinction between combatant and non-combatant.

A third general principle of Murray's formulation of the theory is the legitimacy of defense preparations, and this is justified by two reasons. First, as a matter of fact, there is no international authority which possesses a monopoly on the use of armed force when there is an international dispute. Second, there exists the fact of violence and the lack of principle in the resolution of disputes. Because of these situations the right to self-defense cannot be denied to any state.

The fourth principle is the disallowance by Pius XII of the validity of conscientious objection. Pius argued that when the government acts in a matter that is not immoral, the citizen may not make appeal to his own conscience as grounds for refusing to give his service.

With this as a framework for a point of departure, Murray then analyzes issues in the application of the theory. Murray argues that the doctrine basically boils down to, especially with reference to the terms of public debate, a statement of limited war.\ The principle of limitation for this is the need of legitimate defense against injustice, which must also take into account that force is a last resort and it is to be used only to repel an injury. For Murray, the critical issue is the setting of a public policy that will enable war to be conducted in a limited fashion because that is the moral problem. Murray spells out this orientation forcefully and clearly in describing how it can be used with respect to evaluating the moral issues in the conducting of nuclear war.

> In other words, since limited nuclear war may be a necessity, it must be made a possibility. Its possibility must be created. And the creation of its possibility requires the work of intelligence, and the development of manifold action, on a whole series of policy levels—political (foreign and domestic), diplomatic, military, technological, scientific, fiscal, etc., with the important inclusion of levels of public opinion and public education. To say that the possibility of limited war cannot be created by intelligence and energy, under the direction of a moral imperative, is to succumb to some sort of determinism in human affairs.[61]

To do this Murray suggests that one must construct a kind of model of limited war in which the relationships between different levels of policy-making is established. For example, one must determine the relationship between foreign policy, military policy, and fiscal policy, among others, and then determine which of these takes priority and what is their inner relationship. The other element in the development of a moral policy on war is to attempt to think through where an armed conflict may occur and how that conflict might be limited in those situations with respect to political intentions and military necessities. Thus, for Murray, the moral problem of conducting a just war is to determine exactly how power is to be used, directed, and limited. This requires the setting of appropriate policy so that correct determinations can be made.

A third element that Murray examines is the role of individual conscience in evaluating the decision of a state to conduct war. Murray basically holds that the just war theory provides a means of moral analysis of the use of force in the legitimate self-defense of a state. To do this one must also take into consideration certain political and military dimensions of the situation, but that in itself does not make a judgment about the morality of the war purely political. As Murray says, "It is a judgment reached within a moral universe, and the final reason for it is of the moral order."[62] The tension then, for Murray, is between what he identifies as the conscience of the laws and the conscience of the individual. He argues that when the decision making process of a community has been used and a decision reached, a preliminary measure of internal authority must be conceded to that decision by the citizens. This orientation assumes that the state is both a moral and a political agent and that when it exercises its decision making power, its decision is binding on the citizens and they should unite behind that decision to implement it. With respect to the evaluation of war, then, the citizen must first concede a degree of justice to the common political decision. If citizens should dissent, the burden of proof for that dissent is upon their shoulders, for they must overcome the decision of the state. The moral tension here is between the appropriateness of the state with respect to decision making power and the recognition that citizens must not surrender their conscience to the state. Stated another way, Murray argues that no political society can grant absolute rights to the individual conscience. He sees this as a type of rank individualism and a misunderstanding of the nature of the political community. On the other hand, the political community must respect the conscience of the individual. This, of course, supposes that the consciences of the citizens are both formed and informed.

For Murray, the just war theory is first of all a means to mediate between two extremes that he saw in American society: absolute pacifism in peacetime and extremes of violence in war. The just war theory provided a means to give some discrimination in the use of force. Second, the just war theory assumes that military decisions are functions of political decisions and that political decisions must be seen as moral decisions. Third, because of political decisions or moral decisions there is a necessity for both the state and the citizen to engage in both public and private reflection upon the morality of a particular use of force in a particular situation. As stated earlier, the primary issue is the limitation of force, not the necessary rejection of it. Thus, for Murray, the critical issue is the informed political-moral debate that must engage both the citizen and the state before a war begins so that one can best determine how that war is to be conducted in a moral fashion. This is premised upon the state's having the right to self-defense but also recognizes that, from a moral point of view, the state may not do whatever it wishes to defend itself.

Murray makes one point that is of particular relevance to today's discussion of the conduct of war, especially with respect to our policy of deterrence. He says, "With us, if deterrence fails, and this massive exchange occurs, that is the end. We have no policy after that, except stubbornly to maintain that it is up to the enemy, and not us, to surrender—unconditionally."[63] In this short sentence, Murray points out an extreme failing of our policy of deterrence: What do we do if it doesn't work? I suspect that for Murray the moral issue here is not the use of a policy of deterrence but the narrowness with which our policy is conceived and its exclusive reliance upon unacceptable levels of force as the linchpin of the strategy. I think he finds this perspective to be problematic because of its narrow and uncritical use of force. But whatever his justification for that statement, I think that Murray has said something here that is of particular significance for our situation and needs to be dealt with seriously as we examine the moral dimension of the conducting of war.

## Paul Hanley Furfey

Paul Hanley Furfey, a priest and sociologist at the Catholic University of America, is the author of numerous books and has been involved in various aspects of Catholic activism. His involvement ranges from his own personal work with the Catholic Worker movement and the establishment of various houses of hospitality and settlement houses to his own social and moral analysis of Catholicism and the culture in which it exists in the many books he has written over several decades. During the course of his career, he has made many significant contributions to the evaluation of moral issues relating to war, the draft, pacifism, and nationalism.

One of his consistent themes has been a critique of exaggerated nationalism, which he defines as placing loyalty to the country above loyalty to God.[64] Exaggerated nationalism is a distortion of patriotism that leads people to engage in war. More importantly, though, Furfey argues that exaggerated nationalism can deaden one's conscience so that what is apparently wrong becomes seen as that which is obviously right. Furfey argues that each individual must evaluate the morality of a particular war but that if one is possessed with the spirit of exaggerated nationalism, this evaluation becomes almost impossible because the individual gives his or her loyalty to the wrong reality—the state.

Furfey does not hesitate in using this insight to evaluate the behavior of the American Catholic bishops during World War II. He criticizes them quite severely for not protesting the saturation bombing of German cities during World War II, as well as for approving the dropping of the atomic bomb on Nagasaki and Hiroshima. He also applies this insight to evaluating the war in Vietnam and basically suggests that loyalty to the country inhibited American Catholics from morally evaluating what was going on. Furfey summarizes this orientation very nicely in his commentary on a statement made by Cardinal Spellman during the Vietnam War:

> Sometimes the morality of a war is not merely overlooked but is positively distorted. In an earlier chapter it was mentioned that Cardinal Spellman once settled the moral problem of the Vietnam War to his own satisfaction by paraphrasing Decatur: "Right or wrong, it's my country." This was clearly an explicit repudiation of Christian morality as the supreme norm of conduct. Yet one may be sure that the cardinal was unaware of this repudiation. Doubtless he simply repressed the thought that Decatur's principle was

the negation of Christian moral doctrine. Thus he was able to agree with the super patriots without being conscious of any disloyalty to Catholic teaching. This attitude is doubtless quite common. In wartime, without doubt many Catholics follow the principle that whatever the government commands is the citizen's duty, and they follow this principle without being consciously disloyal to the moral teaching of their Church.[65]

Furfey gives two reasons why Catholics surrender their conscience to the state. First, they tend to accept a popular code of morality which focuses on private sins to be avoided rather than virtues to be practiced. And because this code defines the sins to be avoided in terms of individual morality, the tradition has never clearly articulated a social code of morality or shown how various virtues could lead to social action. Second, moral theology did not develop a strong sense of social sins or social virtues which were obligatory for all people and, therefore, individuals turned to the state by virtue of its laws or its governmental decisions to obtain their code of social morality. Since Christians were now taking their lead of what to do or not do from the state, it should come as no surprise that the state's requirements were not submitted to moral analysis. Political actions and judgments were not seen as appropriate objects of moral analysis.

Furfey continues this analysis in his evaluation of war: "The usual failure to apply Christian principles to public issues is particularly evident in time of war. Few persons are willing to face the elementary truth that war is a moral problem, that a war may be either just or unjust, and that it is the Christian's duty to refuse to support a war when he is morally certain that it is unjust."[66]

In saying this, Furfey is not defining himself as a pacifist. In fact, interestingly enough in an early book he argues: "It is certain beyond any doubt that a Catholic cannot be a conscientious objector in the sense of the absolute pacifists. In other words, no Catholic may assert *a priori* that all wars are wrong and announce his intention of abstaining from any war at all regardless of the issues involved."[67] He also argues elsewhere that non-violence is not to be a substitute for the ordinary agencies of law enforcement and that non-violence is not a universal principle, but a characteristically Christian policy.[68]

According to Furfey, Christianity does not mean the repudiation of physical force under all circumstances: "In the New Testament there is no suggestion that they [Christians] should put down their arms and allow anarchy to prevail."[69] However, Furfey does suggest that non-violence, which he defines as the absence of retaliation when it is to be expected, is a characteristic Christian technique for modifying the social order. Importantly here, he defines it as a strategy as opposed to philosophy of life.

Although not a pacifist, Furfey is very insistent that Catholics take seriously the obligation to morally evaluate war. He uses the tradition of the just war theory for his analysis, but what is different about his approach is that he takes many of the issues seriously and applies them not only to the conduct of the enemy but also to the conduct of his own nation. This approach led him to see World War II and the Vietnam War as unjust wars because of the way in which they were conducted. He logically argues that if individuals morally evaluate the decision of the government to fight a war or examine the conduct of their government while fighting a war and find moral problems, then they are obliged to be conscientious objectors to that particular war. Interestingly enough, Furfey does not limit his notion of an obligation to object to the war only to those who are subject to the draft, for he also puts this obligation upon others whom he calls civilian conscientious objectors. Thus he pursues with logical and moral relentlessness the obligation of a Christian to oppose immoral governmental policies, especially during the conduct of war, regardless of an individual's social position.

While Furfey is not a pacifist, does not accept the opinion that all war is wrong, and continues to use the just war categories as a means of analysis, he also puts a high priority, from a Christian point of view, on a strategy of non-violence as well as demanding a rigorous application of Christian moral principles to the actions and policies of a government. Such an orientation leads him, from a practical point of view, to argue that almost no war conducted in a present context could be viewed as just.

## Dorothy Day and the Catholic Worker

The Catholic Worker movement continues to be an important source of the articulation of concern for the needs of the poor as well as for a continuing critique of society and government policies. Founded by Peter Maurin and Dorothy Day, the Catholic Worker provided houses of hospitality where the poor could find food and shelter and furnished an example of how Christianity could be practiced when taken seriously. The Catholic Worker houses in both urban and agricultural areas were to be viewed as exemplary communities which would provide a vision of Christianity for the rest of the Catholic community. This unique social movement came about as the result of a meeting of Maurin and Day. Day had a history of association with socialists and other radicals during the early 1900s. She had extended sessions of traveling and living with the poor and seeing what kind of life-style they had to endure, as well as a career of journalism and writing. She was dissatisfied to some extent with her life, though, and did not find a direction in it until after the birth of her daughter when she began to see that many of her hopes and aspirations would be fulfilled in Catholicism. But here, too, her hopes were not fulfilled until she met Peter Maurin, a French peasant and wandering teacher. Maurin had been developing his own vision of Christianity, and, in combination with Dorothy Day, this vision was able to be articulated and given a concrete form in the newspaper *The Catholic Worker,* in the various houses of hospitality, and in the concrete forms of social action that were undertaken.

Patricia McNeal suggests that there are three basic touchstones that formed the heart of the Catholic Worker vision. First, there was a type of eschatological radicalism which suggested that the vision and goals of the Catholic Worker movement with respect to the harmony and union of all people could only be achieved at the end of time when Christ would return. The followers of the movement were to live in expectation of this event and were to live it out in their life-style. Second, a sense of Christian personalism was developed which focused on putting love into practice in the arena of history and emphasizing a Christian's ability to turn from being captured by the reality of the world and turning to the reality of the spirit. Third, there was a consistent critique of both nationalism and capitalism which was based on a sense of a nation built around competition and the glorification of struggle. Although it is unclear whether Maurin himself was a pacifist, Dorothy Day argued that pacifism flowed clearly from the principles that they had articulated and was the fulfillment of their vision.[70]

Another important dimension of the Catholic Worker orientation to pacifism was its reading of the events in the late 1930s and early 1940s. The members felt, as did many other individuals, that the developing sources of war were simply a replay of the causes of World War I and that the war would be used to protect the investments of bankers and to develop profits for capitalists and industrialists, and that it would be encouraged by communists and other visionaries who saw war as a means of overthrowing current political structures to set up ones that would advance their ideology.[71]

The general anarchistic philosophy of the Catholic Worker movement, drawing on both Christian and political sources, also led to several practical consequences of its pacifist stance. Its general orientation was to try to have as few interactions with the institutions of the state as possible. This had significant consequences with respect to not paying taxes, and it also led to advancing the idea that individuals should not even register for the draft and should find other ways of avoiding cooperation with the entire structure set up to enlist people in the war machine.

More importantly, the pacifism and non-violence of the Catholic Worker movement and Dorothy Day was based on its Christian vision and sense of personalism which took seriously the command to love one's enemies. The Catholic Worker movement tried to live out as faithfully as possible this unique moral principle in Christianity by not cooperating with violence and by not harming other people. Dorothy Day saw no way to go but that of pacifism and non-violence. Although it originally set out in the context of the just war theory and was, technically, more of a form of selective conscientious objection, nonetheless the Catholic Worker movement began to base its position more and more clearly upon the Gospel injunction of loving one's neighbor and not harming one's enemy and basing its claim to pacifism on that. This stand, articulated in its paper, caused the movement a considerable degree of pain as well as a loss of membership, particularly during World War II. Not all of the members of the loosely associated houses of hospitality bought the idea of pacifism to the same extent Dorothy Day did. Consequently many people left the Worker movement because of the theology of Dorothy Day and because of her acceptance of total pacifism. Some reconciliation was achieved after World War II, but Dorothy Day maintained her insistence that those who subscribed to the movement must also subscribe to pacifism.

Dorothy Day's total acceptance of Christianity and her living out of it in both a life and a strategy of non-violence led her to take positions and support people which made her unpopular in many circles. Her stand was not without a significant cost and seemed many times to put her at the mercy of those who would take advantage of her. Nevertheless, Dorothy Day remained faithful to her principles of pacifism, and she sought to keep the Catholic Worker movement as a sign of how one could both be a pacifist and live in a contemporary society. The movement she established continues to serve, even after her death, as a sign of hope to people who wish to pursue peace and who wish to make non-violence a viable strategy and philosophy of life.

## Thomas Merton

A recent book, picking up on how Merton described himself, calls him "a prophet in the belly of a paradox." Thomas Merton clearly was at least a paradoxical figure: a monk, but an activist; a contemplative, yet an astute political commentator; removed from the world, but having tremendous social influence through his writings and letters; and, finally, not a pacifist, but totally against modern war.

Merton's contribution to the moral analysis of war is very significant. This section will focus on why Merton did not consider himself a pacifist, his moral analysis of war, his reflections on nuclear war, and a summary of his own perspective on peace-making and war-making.

Merton asserted quite clearly: "If a pacifist is one who believes that all war is always morally wrong and always has been wrong, then I am not a pacifist."[72] Such a position, however, did not prohibit him from becoming a non-combatant conscientious objector during World War II nor from conducting a very strenuous moral analysis critiquing the continued reliance on war and violence as a means of achieving peace. A more nuanced version of his thought is the following statement:

> Characteristic of theological thought, both Protestant and Catholic, is the idea that *the presence of nuclear weapons does nothing to alter the traditional just war theory.* I am not a "pacifist" in the sense that I would reject even the *theory* of the just war. I agree that even today a just war might *theoretically* be possible. But I also think we must take into account a totally new situation in which the danger of any war escalating to all-out proportions makes it imperative to find other ways of resolving international conflicts. In practice the just war theory has become irrelevant.[73]

Thus Merton might fall under the label of those who are called nuclear pacifists—those individuals who argue that the presence of nuclear weapons has made it impossible for any war to be just because of the destructive power of nuclear weapons that would be used in that war.

The fact that Merton does not see pacifism as a moral obligation does not mean that he is indifferent to the moral obligation of all Christians to be peacemakers:

> It must however be stated quite clearly and without compromise that the duty of the Christian as a peacemaker is not to be confused with a kind of quietistic inertia that is indifferent to injustice, accepts any kind of disorder, compromises with error and with evil, and gives in to every pressure in order to maintain "peace at any price." The Christian knows well, or should know well, that peace is not possible on such terms. Peace demands the most heroic labor and the most difficult sacrifice. It demands greater heroism than war. It demands greater fidelity to the truth and a much more perfect purity of conscience.[74]

Such an orientation puts a severe moral obligation on the conscience of each Christian to engage in pursuing peace and rejecting
the seduction and illusions of survival that are presented by those
who think that our survival lies with war and the pursuit of the
means that can be used in war. Merton also provides a fairly consistent and thorough critique of contemporary war, especially nuclear
war.

Again we must keep in mind that on a theoretical level Merton
did not rule out the possibility of the use of violent means to defend
oneself or the possibility of engaging in war. However, on a practical
level, he fairly well ruled out the use of war. It is clear that he argued
that total war was immoral: "It is the unanimous judgment of *all*
really serious religious, philosophical, social psychological thought
today that *total war* (whether nuclear or conventional) is both immoral and suicidal. This is so clear that it seems to require little discussion or proof."[75] Merton further argues that even the theologians
who still argue that war itself can be a solution to international conflict agree that total war must be condemned not only as immoral
but also as impractical and eventually self-defeating. He also restates
the issue by saying that it is not simply the case that atomic and nuclear weapons are immoral, but rather that any use of terrorism or
total annihilation is unjust no matter what weapons are employed to
carry out that policy.

Merton further specifies why the just war category is irrelevant:

> The Popes have not merely been trying to say that nuclear
> war is not nice, but that it upsets traditional Catholic
> norms of morality of war. In plain language this is an es-
> sentially new kind of war and one in which the old concept
> of the "just war" is irrelevant because the necessary condi-
> tions for such a war no longer exist. A war of total annihi-
> lation simply cannot be considered a "just war," no matter
> how good the cause for which it is undertaken.[76]

Merton also gets at the issue of the position of the Catholic
Church on nuclear war:

> It is commonly said, even by Catholics, that "the Church
> has never condemned a nuclear war," which is completely

false. Of course the Pope has never pronounced an *ex cathedra* definition which would formally outlaw nuclear
war. Why should he? Does every *infima species* of mortal
sin need to be defined and denounced by the extraordinary
magisterium? Do we now need an *ex cathedra* fulmination
against adultery before Catholics will believe themselves
bound in conscience to keep the sixth commandment?
There is no need for nuclear war to be solemnly outlawed
by an extraordinary definition. It should not even need to
be condemned by the ordinary papal teaching. In fact,
however, it has been so condemned.[78]

Merton used the occassion of an essay on Adolf Eichmann to
make one of his more perceptive and sharp comments about war and
the decision making process involved in launching nuclear weapons:

It is the sane ones, the well-adapted ones, who can without
qualms and without nausea aim the missiles and press the
buttons that will initiate the great festival of destruction
that they, *the sane ones,* have prepared. What makes us so
sure, after all, that the danger comes from a psychotic getting into a position to fire the first shot in a nuclear war?
Psychotics will be suspect. The sane ones will keep them
far from the button. No one suspects the sane, and the sane
ones will have *perfectly good reasons,* logical, well-adjusted
reasons, for firing the shot. They will be obeying sane orders that have come sanely down the chain of command.
And because of their sanity they will have no qualms at all.
When the missiles take off, then, *it will be no mistake.*[79]

Merton quite appropriately attacks the concept of sanity that allows continued discussions of nuclear war to occur and in his sarcas-
tic way begins to expose and undermine the mind set that allows
such thinking to both occur and to be perceived as sane. The problem that he indicates is that we are taking our concept of sanity from
our society, and although that has been done in the past, it is becom-

ing clear that Christians can no longer define sanity in a way that other members of the society do.

It was such a dedication to Christian sanity that led Merton deeper and deeper into the reality behind Christianity and consequently to deepen his commitment to peace and to non-violence as both a philosophy and a strategy. While he had frequent concerns about the direction in which the peace movement was going in the United States, particularly during the Vietnam War and especially when individuals began burning themselves to death as a protest against that war, yet he realized that the direction was the correct one, and he pursued his own efforts at promoting peace-making and continued his writing, even though he was silenced for this for a time by his own superiors. His fidelity to the cause of peace and his eloquent wisdom remain with us as a magnificent legacy from the solitude of Thomas Merton.

### Daniel Berrigan

Among those individuals who captured the imagination of many in the peace movement during the Vietnam War were the brothers Berrigan. These two men, brothers, priests, and members of religious orders, succeeded in articulating a vision of peace and escalation of the strategy of non-violence to include the pouring of blood and napalm on draft records and establishing the mode of a fugitive from prison as a symbol of resistance to unjust authority. While both brothers have been extremely active in the peace movement and continue to be so, this section will focus primarily on Daniel.

Daniel Berrigan has a long tradition of involvement in a variety of social activities, especially as they relate to poor people and minority groups. Also, early in his training he was exposed in Europe to the Worker Priest Movement which had a tremendous impact on his own thinking. In the early 1960s he took part in the freedom rides to achieve the integration of the interstate buses. He also was involved to a large degree in the developing liturgical movement which again, theologically, had a significant influence on his own thought insofar as he saw that the liturgy was a sacrament through which the mystery of humanity's redemption might be acted out and achieved. Finally, Berrigan was eventually exiled to Latin America so that he could be removed from his activities in New York; unfortunately, this proved to further radicalize him, as he was put in contact with many radical groups in Latin America and saw new possibilities for resistance and new justifications for undertaking resistance to the government here.

Two other influences that were very significant for Berrigan—in addition to the ongoing presence of his brother Phillip—were the Catholic Worker movement and Thomas Merton. It is interesting that we find in Daniel Berrigan a coalescing of these two other strands of thought within Catholicism: the social apostolate and the critique of society from a monastic viewpoint. Berrigan had long been involved with the Catholic Worker movement and was influenced significantly by its vision of work with the poor, its pacifism, and its confrontation with the powers of state. And it was at a retreat conducted by Thomas Merton that Berrigan began to develop his own theology of resistance.

Berrigan's journey into civil disobedience and his rejection of many of the institutions of the United States, including the judicial and the executive branches, began out of a sense of frustration that he had exhausted all of the legitimate and traditional means that were at his disposal. He continued to speak, to write, and to engage in traditional acts of non-violent protest, but to no avail. He also saw that the evil present in society, especially as this related to the poor, minorities, and the conduct of the war, was increasing. Finally, after continuing conversations with his brother Phillip as well as his own reflection and prayer, he saw that he had to act and began by his participation in the draft board raid at Catonsville, Maryland. His journey into civil disobedience continued when he realized that he could not in conscience submit to the power that wished to have him go to jail, because he saw that power as an unjust power, one focusing on evil rather than on good. He felt that he could not submit and thereupon undertook the role of a cleric in hiding. He was pursued by the FBI for several months before he was captured and sentenced to jail.

Berrigan continues in much the same vein by living a life of service to his fellow humans. He has worked with dying patients in a cancer hospital, he has continued to write poetry and theological reflections upon the state of America, and he has continued to engage in acts of resistance to the growing militarization of this country. In many ways he has become a thorn in the side of America because he refuses to stop speaking. He refuses to let people forget that they are in danger of being destroyed both by their own complacency as well as by their own compliance with the war machine that seeks to destroy. Berrigan serves as a continual witness to the evil that is present in our culture and society and continues to call all members of the society to a life-style of non-violence.

Daniel Berrigan has, as evidenced in his writings, undergone a most remarkable and dramatic transformation of thought and person. His early writings, the spirit of which is best captured in his first major book *The Bride,* almost see the Church as outside the human world.[80] He is wrestling with the problem of the relationship between the Church and the world, and at this early period in his development he does not have an easy means of bringing together the sacred and the secular. This more transcendent view of the Church is modified in his later development by moving toward seeing the Church as an agent of change and as having a prophetic dimension. The images that he uses at this time suggest that Christians must be a kind of living procession proceeding from the altar into the world and describe the Eucharist as a kind of ferment of redemptive action within humanity.

The liturgy in this perspective is a living out of the law of love within one's place in the world as a means of transforming it. In reliving the mystery of Christ in the liturgy, individuals are to release again into the life around them the energy of God's love and forgiveness which is the power that can redirect us and serve as an agent of our transformation and the transformation of the world. Finally, Berrigan sees that it will be necessary for the Church to take a radical stand of the prophet against society because what the Church sees in society is a radical denial of its message. This vision leads Berrigan to recognize that our faith cannot be our culture, and that our civil citizenship must be different from our membership in the body of Christ. If the Church is to avoid disappearing into the contemporary equivalent of the Roman legions it must be willing to make a clear stand of where its values are and what the practical implications of these are for the life of its members. In his book *No Bars To Manhood* Berrigan says:

No, God implies, there are times so evil that the first and indeed the only genuinely prophetic function is to cast down the images of injustice and death that claim man as victim. No, the times were judged by God; evil beyond cure. Only a new beginning would suffice.[81]

For Berrigan, then, there are two elements which serve as the foundation for his activities: the liturgical and biblical. The liturgical dimension presents the goal of the communication of the mystery of the death and resurrection of Jesus to the community so that it can be changed into the new creation. In this sense, social action becomes the exterior expression of the interior reality of the experience of the liturgy: redemption. It is the acting out of the new creation by making it present within the context of one's everyday life. For Berrigan, social action is the concrete living out of the reality of the Eucharist, the transformation of the bread of one's everyday life into the bread of one's eternal life.

The biblical dimension of Berrigan's thought provides the motivation and criteria for his actions. The Christian Scriptures in particular, as well as the writings of the prophets from the Jewish Scriptures, provide both a vision of the kind of actions one can perform as well as the virtues and reality which those actions ought to bring about. The Christian life is to be an acting out of the parables of Jesus, a living out of the Sermon on the Mount, the Christian Scriptures, by declaring certain forms and styles of life to be null and void so that it will be possible to initiate a new creation, a new beginning. Action based on the biblical inspiration can both point to the need for the new beginning as well as begin to initiate it by incarnating the vision and the reality that will make it possible.

Berrigan's literary output continues unabated; his social action continues; his commitment to the cause of peace and non-violence continues. Although he is certainly not the cult figure that once attracted hundreds of thousands of young people to follow the cause of peace, he continues to be a leading spokesperson for the cause of peace in the United States and to focus our attention on what our life-style will bring us if we do not reorder our priorities. In many ways, all of Berrigan's work is but a commentary on the meditation he provided at Catonsville to interpret the significance of the burning of draft files with napalm:

> We shall beyond doubt be placed behind bars for some portion of our natural lives in consequence of our inability to live and die content in the plagued city, to say "peace, peace" when there is no peace, to keep the poor poor, the thirsty and hungry thirsty and hungry. Our apologies good friends for the fracture of good order the burning of paper instead of children the angering of the orderlies in the front parlor of the charnel house. We could not, so help us God, do otherwise. For we are sick at heart our hearts give us no rest for thinking of the Land of Burning Children and for thinking of that other Child of whom the poet Luke speaks.
>
> We have chosen to say with the gift of our liberty if necessary our lives: the violence stops here the death stops here the suppression of the truth stops here this war stops here. Redeem the times.[82]

## J. Bryan Hehir

J. Bryan Hehir is the associate secretary for the Office of International Peace and Justice for the United States Catholic Conference. In that capacity, and also by his own personal writings on ethical issues, Hehir has continued to use the just war theory and specifically apply it to contemporary military and political problems, especially focusing on strategy. While many of his public statements have been made on behalf of the U.S.C.C., nonetheless they do represent his own personal thought. Hehir has identified two moral problems that relate to the conduct of war: (1) Can the taking of human life for political purposes be justified? (2) How can moral doctrines and strategic doctrines be related?

Hehir is of the opinion that the just war theory can answer these questions positively, and in providing his analysis he also enters into a dialogue with another option: pacifism. The question of strategy is of particular importance for Hehir because it is in its strategic policy that a nation states its intention of what it will or will not do and is therefore the means by which choices are shaped for the political leader, and it provides the bases for determining which structural forces will be used to implement the decisions. Because of this, the primary moral problem on which Hehir focuses, and which is relevant for this presentation, is that of deterrence.

Hehir, however, is particularly concerned to affirm the validity and appropriateness of the just war theory. He does this first because of the continued Church tradition of the legitimacy of the use of violent means to defend violation of a state's rights:

> To assert the right of states to defend themselves without providing a moral framework for the assertions is to leave the road open to the indiscriminate use of force. The assertion requires an ethical calculus defining both the legitimate and the limited means which keep the use of force within the moral universe.[83]

Hehir assumes the use of the tradition of the just war in the papal and conciliar teaching, but he also recognizes that it provides the moral logic needed to determine when and how this right of defense may be implemented. He also argues that the just war theory provides a measure of flexibility to respond to a variety of situations. He recognizes that the just war theory begins with premises that are held in common with pacifists: the sacredness of life, the realization that war is not exclusively a technical or political problem, and the necessity of limiting the uses of violence. What Hehir argues here is not only an affirmation of the legitimacy and even appropriateness of force within the Catholic community, but also the necessity of recognizing that these premises can lead to a variety of conclusions, one of which is something that resembles the just war theory. Hehir recognizes the fact of moral pluralism within the Catholic community and in fact illustrates this by the American bishops' teaching on the legitimacy of both conscientious objection and selective conscientious objection to war. He argues that there can be the possibility of both pacifists and just war theorists in the same ecclesial community, but he argues that the same person cannot hold both of these theories simultaneously. He then further heightens the policy dimension of this pluralism by raising the question of what the public position of the Church should be. That in part is answered by his ecclesiology which basically follows Murray's orientation that the Church has a role in setting the terms for the debate of policy. Hehir does not neglect the fact that the Church must speak to its constituency and must occasionally speak a prophetic word. He is more concerned, however, to keep the Church engaged in the process of public debate and policy analysis, and therefore he continues to see the just war theory as an appropriate means by which the Church can engage in public policy discussions.

In testimony before the House Committee on Armed Services with specific reference to the FY 81 Defense Appropriation Act, Father Hehir, on behalf of the USCC, argued that he was unconvinced that a limited nuclear war could be fought within the confines of a just war ethic. He drew the specific conclusion from this premise that the moral priority must be put on the non-use of nuclear weapons and that, therefore, counterforce capability, especially with respect to the development of the MX missile, should not go forward. Because he is unconvinced that a limited nuclear war could be justified, the primary moral question for him is the evaluation of deterrence: the threat to use nuclear weapons.

The critical question that raises itself in the light of this position has to do with deterrence theory. Hehir is aware that the unique moral problem of nuclear weapons is not the use of them but the threat to use them. As he states, "Deterrence is the hard case for policy and the limit case for the ethics of policy."[84]

Hehir identifies three dimensions of the deterrence debate. The first element is the relationship between the intention to act and the execution of an act, and the moral problem is that contemporary deterrence policy is based upon a stated intention to do what a just war ethic could never legitimize—the destruction of large urban areas. The second element recognizes that an ethic of intention has to be fused with an ethic of consequences. This statement captures the moral irony of deterrence policy: the threat of nuclear retaliation and the threat to do that which would be immoral to do is in fact preventing the use of nuclear weapons. To carry through the justification of this dimension, one could use the contemporary discussion based on the expanded use of the principle of proportionality and ar-

gue that there needs to be a degree of flexibility built into the decision making process and that all factors have to be assessed equally,
and that in a complex situation one may use as an analytical structure "the lesser-evil or morally avoidable-unavoidable evil"[85] method
of analysis. This use of proportionality seeks to weigh good effects
and bad effects and then attempts to discern a method by which a
critical moral tension can be maintained. A third element of the moral theory focuses on the way in which the intention to act, the perception of that intention by the enemy, and the possibility of that
perception causing the movement from the intention to action are related. It is this dimension of the deterrence debate that has the potential to cause the highest degree of dystability within the system, but
again, from a morally ironic point of view, a higher perception of the
willingness to act may indeed lead to a greater degree of stability.

Hehir would favor a position of the toleration of some deterrence strategy based on the recognition that the policy in fact has
created a degree of stability and has actually inhibited the use of nuclear weapons. This conclusion should not be seen as an acceptance
of nuclear weapons or of any avoidance of the serious problems connected with them. What Hehir is concerned to have is a means of
conducting a public debate of the use of these weapons. To do this he
uses the just war categories in a sustained and critical fashion so
that he can have a means of connecting with policy debates and a
framework for their moral analysis. His orientation is both reasoned
and reasonable, and he has made substantive contributions to the
policy debate with respect to nuclear warfare and the just war theory
and also to the analysis of the method of the just war theory as a viable means for analyzing moral dilemmas with war in our contemporary situations.

## Charles Curran

Charles Curran, in his teaching, writing and leadership on a variety of issues, has helped members of the Catholic Church see and
respond to a variety of problems and provided a methodological and
theological basis for their response. While he has not focused any
specific work on the problem of war and peace, his own orientation is

important insofar as it attempts to provide a middle ground between an exclusive reliance on either violence or pacifism.

Methodologically, Curran looks at human reality in the light of the basic five Christian mysteries: creation, sin, incarnation, redemption, and resurrection-destiny. This orientation gives him a stable structure through which to view the complexity of situations that face us—especially with respect to public policy. It also provides some control over the kinds of responses that individuals and the Catholic Church make. Because Curran's methodology recognizes the presence of both goodness and evil in the world and accepts the tension that comes from living between the resurrection and the final coming of God's kingdom, his ethical analysis, accepting compromise and balance, may not be as radical or as critical as that of others. While recognizing that moral compromise may sometimes be necessary, he argues that complex situations require complex analysis and response and that a one sided approach may not respond to the issues in a productive way.

Curran does not reject the possibility of either war or revolution. He sees that in our world these may be, in fact, necessary. However, having said that, he insists upon taking seriously the criterion that war indeed be the last resort and that a decision to enter into war or a violent revolution should be made only with the greatest reluctance and concern.[86] He is concerned that war is not always the last resort and that the theory of just war itself has seldom been used to evaluate a declaration of war by one's own country.

Curran is extremely sensitive to the moral evil of killing that occurs during war and sees this as one of the most serious ongoing ethical problems that we must attend to. He recognizes that war makes human life cheap and expendable, and simultaneously generates a love of violence, an insensitivity and hatred to one's neighbor, and feelings of revenge and reprisal.[87] Such feelings tend to guarantee the violation of the rules of morality in the conduct of war itself and do not make the establishment of peace after a war is concluded any easier. While such possibilities, for Curran, do not eliminate the moral possibility of war, they do put stricter demands on conduct within war than other people would and place a higher degree of moral accountability on the process of declaring war.

In setting out his position on nuclear war and nuclear deterrence, Curran says:

> On the basis of discrimination I would be more hesitant to admit the morality of multimegaton weapons. On the basis of proportionality there seems to be no proportion and justification for such massive nuclear weapons with their tremendous destructive power. This argues not only against the massive nuclear weapons but especially against a great number of such stockpiled weapons.[88]

Even though this statement indicates Curran's moral difficulties with nuclear weapons and deterrence policy, his orientation toward a relationality-responsibility model which sees ethical values in relationship to one another while not absolutizing any one value leads him to argue that one can be opposed to nuclear weapons, or even be a nuclear pacifist, but not have to totally reject the possibility of using violence or violence resistance:

> In this imperfect world in which we live, justice and peace do not always go together. As a last resort I see the possibility of violence—more so even when it is used in a limited way by the weak against the strong, as in the case of liberation and revolution.[89]

Nonetheless, even though Curran can justify the use of violence, he is also aware of the dangers involved in accepting its use: an easy justification of violence, a romanticization of violence and the continued danger of escalating its use.

While Curran's methodology, which accepts some form of moral compromise and justifies the possibility of the use of limited forms of violence, will not satisfy everyone, he recognizes the moral dilemmas in which people find themselves and has attempted to develop a methodology that will allow people to respond to those dilemmas in a coherent and conscientious fashion. He has attempted to build safeguards and limitations into his justification of violence, and he recognizes that the entire community—religious and civil—must be a part of the decision making process. While Curran's methodology is tolerant of a certain amount of difference of opinion within the religious community, it provides a way for people with different values and perspectives on war and violence to begin talking with each other in an attempt to work out a common, viable strategy to resolve the moral problem of war.


## Gordon Zahn

Gordon Zahn has been quite consistent in his pacifist stand for several generations now. Early in his life, he became a pacifist—which he claims was partly a consequence of not having been socialized in a traditional Catholic education system—and this led to his being a conscientious objector during World War II. Consequently, he was sent to a civilian public service camp in New Hampshire where he, along with other dissenters, was to engage in work of national significance. However, they spent most of their time attempting to clear a forest of trees that were felled during a storm.

Zahn's career took a significant turn when he entered Catholic University and did both his master's and doctoral work under the direction of Paul Furfey, focusing on the experiences of the camp and the beliefs of those members of the camp. In his teaching, he has focused on the sociology of war and peace and has presented courses and seminars on different aspects of the peace movement. In his scholarly work, Zahn has devoted all of his energies to writing on various aspects of pacifism and its implementation in both Church and civil society. A continuous stream of articles and books have come from Zahn over the past decade which explicate his position as well as critique the policies of our country and other countries for their continued preparations for war and total destruction. Nor have the policies of the Catholic Church been exempted from this critique. Now in retirement, Zahn continues with some teaching, lecturing and writing on pacifism, as well as weekly service in a Catholic draft counseling center in Boston.[90]

Zahn has made two major points in many of his writings. First, he holds that the position of the early Church, that of non-violence and pacifism, was the original position of the Church and ought to remain the official position of the Church. In many ways, Zahn views the history of Christianity from about the third century, at

least with respect to the question of war, as a fall from grace. Many
of his writings attempt to persuade members of the Church and its
leaders to return to this original position which he perceives to be the
authentic position. Second, Zahn has led a massive, critical, and substantive assault upon the just war theory, arguing that it is simply
inapplicable to the modern context of war—if indeed it was ever applicable to any war. In addition to his perception that the just war
theory allows a degree of moral compromise which he finds unacceptable, Zahn nonetheless argues that even as a theory it is unwork-
able because the range of destruction envisioned by modern warfare
cannot be encompassed by the theory and because the socialization
of citizens is so total that they cannot step back to evaluate critically
the policies of their government in terms of the methodology.

Two other interests of Zahn's continue to manifest themselves
in his writings. The first focuses on the use of the Church by the state
in implementing its political decisions. Zahn demonstrated this hy-
pothesis in his work on the Catholic Church's role in supporting the
policies of Nazi Germany in World War II. Other writings suggest
that this orientation is operative in the United States and that the
Church is continuously in danger of being used as a means of social
control by the state in achieving its political goals. The other theme
finds expression in Zahn's work on the role of individual moral decision making. Zahn has done much interesting work in terms of providing an ethical and sociological analysis of conscience and its role
in moral decision making. In many ways this theme comes out of his
own personal experience and the problems he had in acting out his
conscientious decision to oppose war, but it received confirmation
and strength from the work that has brought him personally the
most satisfaction: his work on the Austrian peasant Franz Jaegerstet-
ter. The inspiration of this almost solitary dissenter to Hitler's war
has proven a model of inspiration for both Zahn and many other individuals as they embark on their own conscientious journeys of
evaluation of the policies of different nation-states with respect to
war.

Zahn has been frequently faulted for his single-mindedness and
total commitment to pacifism. He has also been called to task by
many individuals for his linking of pacifism and abortion, based on
his perception that life may not be violated at any stage or in any

way. In a conversation with me, Zahn remarked that he saw no problems with leaving Karen Ann Quinlan on her respirator indefinitely as a sign of respect for life—as long as the family was able to afford such treatment and as long as no one else would need the respirator more. While many see such a position as extreme and even foolhardy, it is consistent with his pro-life position.

Zahn has been one of the primary standard-bearers for both pacifism and a critique of the war policy and strategy of this nation. While many do not agree with him, nonetheless they have been inspired by him and his work to examine more critically the just war theory and the policies of our country. In many ways Zahn is one of the individuals responsible for the resurgence of the viability of pacifism and non-violence in contemporary American Catholicism. His writings certainly have provided the theoretical underpinnings for such an event to occur, and he himself has long been active in various movements and organizations whose work has proven to be effective in having different dimensions of Catholicism re-examine its stand on war. His continued witness to the cause of peace and his willingness to be present at demonstrations and meetings and to engage in constant dialogue with other members of the Church has helped to provide a vision and framework for a re-evaluation of war in contemporary Catholicism. His faithfulness in promoting the cause of peace has certainly been one of the sources that the current critique of war and the promotion of peace relies upon.

# 4
# Contemporary Developments

## The State of the Question

When the Vietnam War ended and the debates, dissent, and rancor that characterized the conduct of that war subsided, the whole nation seemed to quiet down and go into a sort of moral and psychic hibernation. Perhaps the country needed a respite from the intensity and the divisions that the Vietnam War and the previous civil rights debate had brought about in our country. Perhaps people wanted to get on with other dimensions of their lives. Student leaders were entering the marketplace and needed to establish themselves. Families were started and life seemed to continue. Then Watergate came along and began sapping the moral energies of our nation once more. The worst fears of many individuals about government surveillance and cover-ups were realized and played out in the public drama of the Watergate hearings. The issue was probably not so much the actual corruption and cover-up as it was the perception of the pettiness and arrogance of the individuals involved. The nation somehow managed to make it through the resignation of a president, the installation of a president not elected by a national vote, and another presidential campaign without suffering the ultimate throes of despair. Another oil crisis visited itself upon our country and caused other problems. These were heightened by the prolonged captivity of American citizens by Iran. Perceptions and feelings of frustration and despair were mixed by an increasing desire to use less restrained measures to liberate the captives, but this was not to be and we awaited their release for hundreds of agonizing days.

After the perception of the aimlessness of the Carter administration in both domestic and foreign policy, the philosophy of the Reagan administration at least offered a clear alternative. Reagan may have surprised many people by following through on many of his campaign promises, especially those reducing the amount of federal monies made available for various entitlement programs and for increasing the defense budget, while simultaneously lowering taxes. However, it is the policies of the Reagan administration, or perhaps the dues that need to be paid as the result of previous administrations that Reagan has inherited, that have set the context for the current debate about war and peace and the defense budget in our time.

There are two particular issues that are important in this debate. The first is the dramatic nature of the increase of the military budget. Projections call for increasing the budget by over $1,640 billion during the next five years. These budgetary increases were accompanied by an initial hard line on foreign policy and the appearance of being willing to use the weapons at hand if we perceived that the Soviets were stepping out of line. Whether or not the full extent of defense appropriations envisioned by the Reagan administration will come to pass, an increasingly disproportionate amount of funds are being sunk into the military.

The other dramatic reality has to do with the significance and severity of the defunding of various entitlement programs. Again, while many would feel reasonably comfortable in saying that there has been waste in these programs, nonetheless there is a perception that this administration is attempting to dismantle most, if not all, of the social welfare programs of our recent past. One of the many problems in this is that the claim of doing this to decrease the federal budget is not quite true. What is occurring is a massive transfer of funds from one set of accounts, the social welfare accounts, to the military account. Thus while the rhetoric is budget reduction, in effect what we have is the transfer of funds from one line item to another. Another major problem is the genuine hardship being caused by the decrease of funds. At a time of increasing inflation and unemployment, the defunding of many entitlement programs has caused enormous hardship to hundreds of thousands of individuals in our country. The price of the escalating military expenditures is literally coming out of the pockets of the poor.

In our time we are witnessing a renewed concern for peace which is being shown in many ways. First, internationally, there have been many and extremely large demonstrations against the increasing reliance upon nuclear weapons as a means of defending Europe. There is a growing realization that the price of saving Europe through nuclear war will be its destruction. Second, there are a growing number of professionals, primarily following the model set by physicians, who are addressing the issues of nuclear war. Physicians in particular, through the organization Physicians for Social Responsibility, have been firm and clear in their descriptions of the medical consequences of a nuclear war. Their basic argument is that the medical resources of any community are utterly inadequate for responding to the medical consequences of a nuclear war. This argument makes the claim of several administrations that we can survive a nuclear war ring quite hollow. Third, many individuals are refusing to register for the draft. Estimates go as high as eight hundred thousand eighteen-year-olds who have not registered. The other interesting feature in this is that, of those individuals who have registered, large numbers appear not to be notifying the government of any change of address. What this means is that many young people, whether for ideological or other reasons, are not willing to commit themselves to being destroyed for some reason that they may not agree with. Fourth, most important in terms of the concerns of this book, there has been a growing appreciation and articulation of a positive theory of pacifism and non-violence. What is very significant is that pacifism has become a viable option almost enjoying equal status with the tradition of the just war. This orientation very slowly began with Vatican Council II and has now grown to the point where the American Catholic bishops are quite comfortable with accepting selective conscientious objection and are themselves beginning to mount a severe critique of the just war theory and the foreign policy of our country, especially as it relates to nuclear war. Such an orientation or stance by the American Catholic bishops would have been unthought of even in the mid-1970s. Not all, of course, are in agreement with this position, and at least one book has come out arguing that the just war theory is viable and that pacifism is a problematic stance.

It is difficult to identify any issue among the many that have just been mentioned as the critical factor in helping to focus the attention of the broader community, and in particular the Catholic community, and, within that, the American bishops, on the issue of pacifism and the moral problems of nuclear war. One of my senses, however, is that many persons, including the Catholic bishops, were genuinely scandalized by the naming of a first strike submarine with nuclear warheads *Corpus Christi.* Even though this submarine is named after a city, and even though other military vessels have borne the names of saints who have also been the patrons of various cities, and even though the Secretary of the Navy is a Catholic and had done research into the issue of war and peace and determined that the Catholic Church perceives the military force as an instrument of peace, nonetheless I think that there was a genuine sense of moral outrage at both the insensitivity of the navy in naming the submarine *Corpus Christi* and the idea that this submarine could be responsible for the ultimate transubstantiation of the world through a nuclear holocaust. The naming of this submarine is a small and possibly insignificant event in terms of other events of our recent history. Nonetheless I think it raised up a particular orientation and served as a moment of grace in which many individuals saw that the policies we were pursuing with respect to an increasing reliance on nuclear warfare, a rhetoric which made it appear likely that we would use such a force, and the increasing appropriations for the military were at least problematic, if not wrong.

## Responses of the American Catholic Bishops

The National Conference of Catholic Bishops at their November 1981 meeting established an *ad hoc* committee on war and peace, headed by Archbishop Bernardin of Chicago. In a statement describing some of the agenda of that committee, Archbishop Bernardin made several important summary statements relating both to the tradition and to the work of the committee.

Bernardin summarized the four principal contributions of the *Pastoral Constitution on the Church in the Modern World* as follows:

First, in its assessment of scientific weapons of mass destruction, of which nuclear weapons are the principal example, it uttered a clear condemnation. It had condemned attacks on civilian centers and large populated areas as a crime against God and humanity (paragraph 80). Second, it supported the right of conscientious objection, a pacifist position, in the clearest statement we have yet in Catholic teaching. Third, it reasserted the right of nations to acts of legitimate defense, an acknowledgement that some uses of force, under restricted conditions, could be justified. Fourth, it raised but did not resolve the moral issues posed by the doctrine of nuclear deterrence.[91]

He then traced some of the related positions in recent statements of Catholic bishops. One of these has been the emergence of a sort of Catholic pacifism. In addition there has been an acknowledgement of the continuing legitimacy of service in the military as service to society. There has also been the endorsement of the right of conscientious objection and selective conscientious objection. Finally, Archbishop Bernardin highlighted the testimony of Cardinal Krol in 1979 to the Senate Foreign Relations Committee in which he made three interrelated moral judgments:

> First, the primary moral imperative is to prevent any use of nuclear weapons under any conditions. Second, the testimony judges that the possession of nuclear weapons in our policy of deterrence cannot be justified in principle, but can be tolerated only if the deterrent framework is used to make progress on arms limitation and reduction. The third principle, a corollary of the second, is the imperative for the super powers to pursue meaningful arms limitation aimed at substantial reductions and real disarmament.[92]

These considerations have led Archbishop Bernardin to set the following issues as illustrative of the concerns for the committee. First, developing a positive theology of peace which looks beyond limiting the destructive power of war. Second, examining the implications of the stringent limits placed on the use of force in our day by recent Popes. This orientation will look not only at nuclear war but the non-nuclear use of force.

However, Bernardin was careful to note that the moral problem of nuclear war would be the most challenging task and probably the center of attention for the committee. He gave several reasons for this. First, it was the United States which first developed and used atomic weapons. Second, the United States is among the countries which have helped to develop nuclear weapons of greater accuracy and national security strategies around those weapons. Third, there has been an increasing coupling of the use of deterrence with a willingness to fight limited nuclear wars. Fourth, the position taken by American Catholic bishops challenges significantly the United States policy of defense.

How this committee will pull all of the different and differing strands of moral reasoning together in a coherent statement is not clear at the present time. Nonetheless the fact that such a commission has been established and that it will examine the significant moral questions concerning our war and deterrence policy for today is extremely important. In many ways the process of going through such an examination of a moral position with respect to war, and especially nuclear weapons, may be more important than the actual document itself. For what this committee has done is, on the one hand, to validate the questioning of United States foreign policy especially with respect to nuclear weapons and deterrence, and, on the other hand, to recognize the validity and significance of the contributions of the Catholic peace movement of the last several decades.

## Statements of Individual Bishops

Several bishops have made their own statements about war and peace in advance of the report by this committee. Summaries of statements from several bishops follow.

### Bishop Anthony M. Pilla, Cleveland, Ohio

Bishop Pilla phrases his examination of the question of the morality of nuclear war within the context of traditional Christian re-

spect for the sanctity of life and suggests this as the basis for a
Catholic re-evaluation of the questions raised by the awesome power
of nuclear weapons. After presenting a summary of the just war
theory, its applicability to traditional warfare, and a critique of the
bombing of Hiroshima, Pilla then goes on to raise several questions
about nuclear warfare.

The majority of the positive part of Pilla's statement is a reiteration of the teaching of recent Popes and the Vatican Council, as well
as pastoral letters from the American bishops on nuclear warfare.
The general tone and orientation of his statement is that nuclear war
is very difficult to justify and that there are significant problems
raised both by building nuclear weapons and by using them in a policy of deterrence. What is significant about his orientation is that it
picks up on a concern raised by Archbishop Bernardin: the presentation of a positive theology of peace in which the intent of Christian
moral questioning and action is not simply to outlaw war, but to promote and build the structures of justice that will permit peace to
flourish.

Concluding this statement are a number of positive recommendations for acting on some of the Church's teachings about war and
peace. These include, but are not limited to, establishing a peace and
justice committee in each parish, instituting an annual peace week to
promote peace education in the diocese, planning liturgies for national holidays to help raise the awareness of the difference between patriotism and militarism, urging Catholics involved in the production
of weapons of mass destruction to reconsider the moral implications
of working in such places, supporting the establishment of a World
Peace Tax Fund as an alternative to using tax monies for war, helping to train draft counselors, and supporting and participating in the
nuclear freeze campaign.

Bishop Pilla concludes his statement with a very important note
in that he shows how questioning the policy of the government is an
act of patriotism, even if it criticizes what the government is doing:

As the prophets criticized the immorality of the societies in
which they lived, so we must unite to oppose the evils inherent in our own political system. The emphasis placed on

military buildup and weapons proliferation in our country
is one such evil.[93]

## *Archbishop John R. Quinn, San Francisco, California*

Archbishop Quinn used the occasion of the eight hundredth an-
niversary of the patron saint of San Francisco to make a pastoral
statement on the issue of war and peace. He put forward St. Francis
as a prophet of poverty and peace for our own age and used this inspiration to help examine the question of the use of nuclear weapons
and the escalation of the arms race.

Quinn begins his statement by focusing on the moral dilemma
that we face as a consequence of having developed nuclear power: we
have created a military technology without having thought through
its moral implications, or, to rephrase it, we have developed a technology without questioning whether we have the moral capacity to
control the power we had created. Quinn restates this dilemma by
citing Albert Einstein who recognized that the splitting of the atom
had changed everything but our modes of thinking.

Quinn uses this phrase as a way of challenging Christians to rethink our nuclear strategy. He indicates that the United States has a
stockpile of nuclear weapons equivalent to six hundred and fifteen
thousand times the explosive force of the bomb dropped at Hiroshima. This gives the United States an overkill power of about forty. By
contrast, the Soviet Union has only an overkill power of about seven-
teen. Quinn notes that we continue to build three nuclear warheads
per day and that these account for a large part of the hundreds of
billions of dollars which have been budgeted for the Pentagon over
the next five years. He also argues that this spending on weapons is a
form of theft from the poor who have resources that are needed for
their very survival diverted from them to preparation for war.

Quinn begins his presentation of the teachings of the Church by
noting two elements: a recognition of the statement from the Gospel
of Matthew that we shall not kill and a recognition that the Gospel
teaching does not rule out the right of nations to protect themselves
against enemies. Quinn locates the particular moral problem of our
age as occurring when the effects of our defensive weapons are no

longer fully predictable or within our control. He then says that the teaching of the Church is clear: "Nuclear weapons and the arms race must be condemned as immoral."[94] After this he applies the traditional just war principles to nuclear warfare and draws this conclusion:

> If we apply each of these traditional principles to the current international arms race, we must conclude that a "just" nuclear war is a contradiction in terms.[95]

Quinn concludes with the recognition that there will be a diversity of responses to the challenge of the morality of nuclear war within the Catholic community, and he proposes three areas in which Catholics might work together to bring some degree of morality to the situation. First, he invites a monthly day of fast and abstinence as a means of petitioning an end to the arms race. He then recommends a broad-based educational program on the Church's teaching with respect to nuclear warfare throughout the archdiocese. Finally, he asks that Christians find a practical expression in the political and social arenas. Here he presents three specific recommendations. He asks individuals to participate in the national campaign for a nuclear arms freeze. Second, he asks the administrators and staff of Catholic health facilities to join those who are opposing the intentions of the Department of Defense to establish a "civilian-military contingency hospital system" if this system is based on the illusion that there can be an effective medical response in the case of nuclear war. Third, he asks for support for developing creative proposals for converting military weapons technology to civilian productions use.

These last two recommendations are of particular importance insofar as they are suggestions that have not been made publicly by other Catholic bishops. Quinn rightly critiques the contingency hospital system which alleges the survivability of a nuclear war. With respect to the conversion technology, Quinn recognizes that we must use the creativity we have to make this transfer and do so in a way that will enable large numbers of peoples to participate in it. This last recommendation should be of particular importance for Catholics who are engineers and scientists. A particularly unique and wonderful contribution that could be made by these individuals would be to lead the way in developing a genuine conversion technology.

## Bishop L. T. Matthiesen, Amarillo, Texas

Bishop Matthiesen made two different statements that, while not as nuanced or clearly located in the framework of the tradition as the other bishops' statements have been, are nonetheless interesting and significant, especially since they evaluate war and nuclear weapons from a different perspective.

For example, in his testimony on the MX missile, Bishop Matthiesen argued against locating the system in Texas as follows:

> You will crisscross our farms and our ranches with highways and yet more roads; you will uproot families, hundreds and hundreds of them; you will drain our already rapidly decreasing water supply; you will bring in a boomtown atmosphere, then leave us with ghost towns; you will require us to provide services for the work crews, and then tell us you do not need us any longer.[96]

But his most critical argument is that locating the MX system in Texas will make his area a primary target and leave innocent people at the center of a target system. Bishop Matthiesen is careful to note that he does not want the system moved elsewhere. He wants it to be eliminated entirely, for no system which guarantees the destruction of innocent men, women, and children is morally acceptable.

Thus, his critical argument against the locating of the MX system in Texas is simply that it will destroy personal and social life as the people know it and will guarantee that the innocent will be placed in jeopardy.

Bishop Matthiesen also spoke on the subject of the production and stockpiling of the neutron bomb, and again his comments are not located within the tradition of the just war theory, for he approaches the issue from a different and morally interesting perspective. He argues that the development of the neutron bomb reveals that the military can—and he says perhaps must—think in only one way: each enemy advance in arms technology and capability must be met with a further advance on our part. He then suggests that we turn our energies from this destructive use to the peaceful uses of nuclear energy and attempt to use them to produce food, fiber, clothing, shelter and transportation, and, in a move that caused particular anguish for several people in his diocese, he proposes:

> We urge individuals involved in the production and stockpiling of nuclear bombs to consider what they are doing, to resign from such activities, and to seek employment in peaceful pursuits.[97]

While he did not mandate that individuals resign their jobs, he certainly gave the strong impression that such employment was morally inappropriate and that from his perspective it would be wrong for individuals to continue in such employment.

Such a recommendation raises another moral dimension of nuclear warfare: the responsibility civilians have to evaluate morally their employment. Most of the just war criteria have focused on the state and the military; Matthiesen's recommendations raise the issue of what moral responsibilities civilians have as they pursue their livelihood. This question is especially difficult not only from the critical moral perspective but also from a practical perspective. As unemployment rates continue to rise and the military budget continues to increase dramatically, it is clear that many job opportunities will be found in defense-related plants and that many individuals will have to choose between employment that is morally problematic and no employment and, consequently, no support for their families. This problem has been addressed through the establishment of the Solidarity Peace Fund, funded by the Oblates of Mary Immaculate, to help employees who, for reasons of conscience, have resigned from the Pantex plant where nuclear weapons are produced.

## Archbishop Raymond G. Hunthausen, Seattle, Washington

Bishop Hunthausen made several significant statements with respect to nuclear weapons, especially the Trident system. Like Bishop Matthiesen of Texas, he does not use the categories of the just war as a means of articulating his moral opposition.

At the heart of Hunthausen's opposition to nuclear war is his perception of the teaching of the call to carry the cross, present in the heart of the Gospel of Mark. He says that we cannot think about our call to carry the cross in abstract terms, but must think about it as a call to love God and one's neighbor in a direct way. This means that in our age, from Hunthausen's perspective, we must take up the cross of unilateral disarmament and risk living without the alleged security of nuclear weapons:

> Our security as people of faith lies not in demonic weapons which threaten all life on earth. Our security is in a loving, caring God. We must dismantle our weapons of terror and place our reliance on God.[98]

Hunthausen then discusses two dimensions of a policy of unilateral disarmament. First, he presents the moral irony that we are more terrified by talk of disarmament than we are about the risks and consequences of nuclear war. This is related to the fact that nuclear arms protect privilege and exploitation, and giving them up implies relinquishing our economic power over other nations and peoples. Divesting ourselves of nuclear weapons requires a change in our economic policies, a reality attended to by few commentators. He says then that "giving up the weapons would mean giving up more than our means of global terror. It would mean giving up the reason for such terror—our privileged place in the world."[99]

A second suggestion that Hunthausen makes is to engage in tax resistance by withholding fifty percent of one's taxes:

> Form 1040 is the place where the Pentagon enters all of our lives and asks our unthinking cooperation with the idol of nuclear destruction. I think the teaching of Jesus tells us to render to a nuclear-armed Caesar what that Caesar deserves—tax resistance, and to begin to render to God alone that complete trust which we now give, through our tax dollars, to a demonic form of power. Some would call what I am urging "civil disobedience." I prefer to see it as obedience to God.[100]

This dramatic statement by a Catholic bishop caused a significant amount of commentary and, to say the least, raised eyebrows in
some circles. This led Hunthausen to issue a second statement which
clarified but reiterated his original statement. This second statement
makes several other significant points. First, he argues that all nuclear war is immoral because there is no conceivable proportionate reason which could justify the destruction of life and resources that the
war would entail. Then he says that since the arms race makes nuclear war inevitable, participation in it is also immoral. He therefore
concludes that unilateral disarmament is the only moral position
possible in our age.

In addition to this basic clarification and clear statement of his
moral position, Hunthausen also took this opportunity to state four
other issues that are related to his position on nuclear war and tax
resistance. First, he stated that he has the right and duty to speak out
on the concrete issues of the day as they affect Catholic morality. He
suggests that statements by a bishop should be specific and attempt,
to the best of that bishop's ability, to apply the Gospel to daily living.
Second, Hunthausen rejected the notion that because the episcopal
office is a religious office a bishop should not speak out on political
issues. Third, he reiterated his suggestions about tax resistance but,
more importantly, argued against those who thought that it is immoral to disobey the law of the state for a good end. He showed the
relation of the tradition of civil disobedience to traditional Roman
Catholic theology and argued that it is more important to be faithful
to the laws of God than the laws of the state. Fourth, he argues that
every nation has a moral obligation to bring about peace and disarmament and not to make itself the strongest nation on earth. He
says: "Any nation which makes as its first priority the building up of
armaments and not the creative work of peace and disarmament is
immoral." In another statement Hunthausen presents other comments on the use of nuclear weapons which are further articulations
of his understanding of the moral problem of nuclear war, as he asserts: "A nuclear first-strike weapon is the ultimate violation of both
God's law and international law." For him this is the basis on which
he condemns the Trident missile. He is also helpful in unmasking
some of the moral reality hidden behind descriptions of such weapon
systems by the Pentagon:

Pentagon planners have cloaked the reality of first-strike in such terms as 'counterforce' and countervailing strategy, whose meaning is in fact the pre-emptive destruction of enemy deterrent forces together with millions of innocent people designated by strategists as "collateral civilian damage."[101]

A second comment that he makes and is, in some ways, a development of other comments is that he would hope that we could learn to make peace through non-violence with the same degree of sacrifice as those who seek peace through war:

Non-violence requires at least as much of our lives as war does. The truth is found in Jesus' non-violent teaching of the cross: to lay down our lives out of love, not while taking the lives of others but by revering them more deeply. Our reverence for life needs to deepen to that truth at the cross where the God of love calls us to give up our lives for life itself.[102]

Perhaps the depth of Hunthausen's moral concern and outrage is summarized best in his statement that "Trident is the Auschwitz of Puget Sound." While that statement is extremely strong and probably very troublesome to many people, it nonetheless represents the conclusion of a rather significant and detailed working through of a moral position on nuclear war. Finally, Hunthausen has recently demonstrated the depth of his commitment by announcing his withholding of fifty percent of his federal tax to protest our war policy. Such a dramatic gesture, unprecedented in American Catholicism, both opens the way to a re-evaluation of this nation's nuclear policies and suggests a new strategy of resistance.

## Cardinal Cooke, New York

Cardinal Cooke's letter to military chaplains is different than the other messages we have looked at insofar as it is directed to a very specific audience: the Catholic chaplains in the United States armed services. This letter is motivated by two major concerns: first, many Catholic men and women in the miltary service have been asking questions with respect to the morality of war and peace, with special emphasis on nuclear weapons; second, bishops have a special obligation to present the moral teaching of the Catholic Church to help form the consciences of its members, and this letter is an attempt to do this.

In this letter, Cooke addresses two major questions: Has the Church changed its position on military service? Must a Catholic refuse to have anything at all to do with nuclear weapons?

The first question is answered very quickly and simply by reiterating the statement from the document *The Church in the Modern World* which says:

> All those who enter the military service in loyalty to their country shall look upon themselves as the custodians of the security and freedom of their fellow countrymen; and when they carry out their duty properly, they are contributing to the maintenance of peace.[103]

The second question is answered in a lengthier and more nuanced fashion. Cooke uses three principles to justify the participation of Catholics in areas of the armed service that involve nuclear weapons. First, he repeats the tradition of the Catholic Church that a government has the right and duty to protect its people against unjust aggression. The implication of this is that a country can develop and maintain weapon systems to try to prevent war by deterring another nation from attacking it. Second, the Church recognizes that as long as we have reason to believe "that another nation would be tempted to attack us if we could not retaliate, we have the right to deter attack by making it clear that we *could* retaliate."[104] Cooke argues that government leaders have a moral obligation to come up with alternatives to deterrence, but as long as we are sincerely trying to work with other nations to find a better way, the Church considers the strategy of nuclear deterrence morally *tolerable.* Third, he then concludes that if the strategy of nuclear deterrence is morally tolerated, those who produce or are assigned to handle the weapons that make the strategy possible can do so in good conscience.

Cooke also raises the question that a nation must daily ask itself:

"How much defense is enough? How much is too much?" He recognizes that a nation must use its resources on behalf of all its citizens but suggests that we may not assume that reductions in defense would solve automatically problems like poverty, hunger and disease. While recognizing the nation's obligation to provide for different needs of its citizens, Cooke concludes that there would be "little point in a nation's spending all its resources on feeding, clothing, housing and educating the poor, and on other needs, only to leave all its people defenseless if attacked."[105]

Cooke concludes his letter to the chaplains by announcing the establishment of a House of Prayer and Study for Peace. This house will be under the supervision of the Vicar General of the Military Vicariate, and the board of advisors will include "men and women representing a broad spectrum of occupations and disciplines." The daily activities of prayer and study will be supported and carried out by a small staff of religious and lay persons and residents in the house itself. Choosing as a theme for the house Pope Paul VI's statement "If you wish peace, defend life," the staff will attempt to pool a variety of resources and share findings about war and peace and try to encourage individuals to join in prayer that peace with justice will be a reality within our lifetime.

What is interesting about this letter from Cardinal Cooke, in comparison to some of the other statements of bishops that we have examined, is its fairly close reliance on the just war theory. While this is neither wrong nor inappropriate, its use gives a significantly different tone and feel to this document. Another important issue in this statement is how Cooke presents the issue of nuclear deterrence. He moves very quickly from the justification of a general strategy of deterrence to defending a strategy of nuclear deterrence. While I would agree that one can find support for a position of nuclear deterrence within the Church, what I find missing in Cooke's statement is a reasoned presentation of why that occurs. It seems to me that he moves too quickly from a general affirmation of a deterrence policy. It would be helpful, and the document would be more coherent, if there were some elaboration of the justification process. Finally, the letter ends on a positive tone with the establishment of the House of Prayer and Study and the linking of the protection of life to other social issues, in particular the newborn, the elderly, the poor and the hungry. Such a linking of an affirmation of the value of life to social policy is, I think, a very helpful move and may serve to lead to a very serious moral examination of a variety of social policies in our country.

### Bishop John J. O'Connor, Vicar General, Military Vicariate, New York

Bishop O'Connor is the author of a book entitled, *In Defense of Life*[106] which purports to clarify the official Catholic Church teaching on the just war theory. O'Connor focuses on three questions: Is it possible to have a just war today? Can the use of nuclear weapons ever be justified? Is conscientious objection a right, a duty, neither or both? What is interesting about this book is not the answers to these questions, but the methodology used to answer them. The answers are presented fairly succinctly. Yes, it is possible to have a just war today. If by nuclear weapons we mean strategic weapons of mass destruction, no, we may not use them. If we understand nuclear weapons to be tactical nuclear weapons or nuclear weapons not of massive destruction, the answer is that perhaps we may justify their use. Finally, O'Connor recognizes that a Catholic may be a conscientious objector when circumstances warrant. However, he notes that the Church has not come down overwhelmingly on the side of the conscientious objector as the norm with military service as an exception.

This methodology by which O'Connor gets to these conclusions is extremely interesting, but exceedingly problematic. In this section I will indicate several problems with the methodology which will explain many of my misgivings about his conclusions. First, he identifies the Church exclusively with the hierarchy. It is true that the hierarchy is an extremely important part of the Roman Catholic Church, but contemporary theology, and even traditional theology, would recognize that the Church is composed of more members than the hierarchy. In conjunction with the tradition of looking toward the belief of the people as a source of morality, one must necessarily look beyond the hierarchy to understand who and what the Church is.

Second, with respect to his statement of the Church's teaching, O'Connor looks only to papal, conciliar, and episcopal conference documents, with an occasional nod to the statements of the ordinary of a particular diocese. Again, the statements of these groups are extremely important and serve as a kind of bellweather for reading Catholic opinion about a particular topic. Nonetheless, there is a vast theological literature on war and peace not alluded to in the examination of the issues of the book. In fact, in a surprising statement, O'Connor says: "Again it is worth recalling that even though nuclear weaponry has been publicly known for some thirty-five years, professional moralists have still not provided the analyses or the body of literature similar to that available in medical ethics or other fields."[107] That statement, I think, represents a significant lack of awareness of contemporary literature of the just war theory and the literature on ethical dimensions of modern warfare. Perhaps the fact that O'Connor believes that one does not need to look beyond the hierarchy to understand the teaching about war and ethical issues of nuclear warfare leads to his making that statement.

A third issue that is of particular importance with respect to his methodology is his discussion of those individuals he labels as the "neo-Gnostics." These are individuals "who in their zeal to avert war and to condemn the things of war tend to convey the impression that their personal convictions, and only theirs, reflect the true teachings of Christ."[108] A new revelation has been given to them. Whatever the Church may have taught in the past, it could not be the *true* Church, or the Church of true *Christians,* were it to tolerate war under any circumstances in the future. These neo-Gnostics do three things that trouble O'Connor. First, they urge individuals to follow their consciences regardless of mandates from civil authorities. Second, they lose a hearing from the more thoughtful advocates of peace in the courts of military planners and government decision makers. Third, they distract society from objectively studying the totality of discernible facts, the understanding of which is essential to the formulation of a rational response to world events and perceived provocations to war.

The major problem in responding to these claims is, first, that O'Connor never identifies who these people are. Consequently, one cannot even refer to their arguments to evaluate his claims. Second, the three reasons that O'Connor uses to argue why these "neo-Gnostics" are problematic are basically *ad hominem* and gratuitous assertions. He does not present an argument justifying the correctness of his perceptions about these individuals and their alleged stances, nor does he show that these three things are the core of the issue of the evaluation of whoever these individuals might be. A third critique of his use of this particular category is that it reflects a continuation of his bias against reading authors and commentators who are not members of the hierarchy.

The most serious failure in O'Connor's entire presentation, though, is his use of an outmoded ecclesiology and an exclusive reliance on the worst kind of ecclesiastical positivism to make his claim. The bottom line question for O'Connor is: Has any Pope ever said that it is a sin to participate in war? The answer to that obviously is "no," but one has to ask if that is the appropriate methodological question and if that is the only norm for evaluating what is sinful in Catholic moral theory. I would personally hate to construct a code of moral theology based on only those things that Popes have said specifically were sinful. Such an orientation misses major segments in Catholic moral theology, including, but not limited to, Scripture, tradition, theological discussion, and the belief of the community.

O'Connor ends his book with a pro-life appeal. What is interesting to me is that he uses an anti-abortion argument as some sort of a justification for continuing a policy of nuclear deterrence and reliance upon war as a means of vindicating rights. This is a tentative conclusion on my part because it is really unclear to me what O'Connor is arguing for in his last chapter. It is a very strong pro-life statement, buttressed by appropriate papal and episcopal quotations, but I do not see clearly how this relates to his previous discussion or how it might relate to an analysis of war. Would he, for example, want to go as far as Gordon Zahn and suggest that those who are anti-abortion should also by virtue of logical consistency be anti-war. I think not. What needs to be done is to make clear the connection that he is drawing between pro-life and the viability of the just war theory.

In its insistence to justify a particular position by reliance on a highly selective use of papal statements, it seems to me that O'Connor's book represents either the last gasp of the just war theory to try to justify the military policies of our present administration or the thought of an individual who simply has missed the focus and direction of papal and theological thought and commentary since John

XXIII. Clearly no Pope has said that it is a sin to fight in a war, and all Popes of recent years have recognized that nations retain the right of self-defense. But what is more important to recognize is that there has been a considerable shift in attitude which has made the justification of war, the arms race, and nuclear deterrence more difficult. Recent papal statements, letters of bishops, and conclusions of theologians reveal a strong affirmation of a theology of peace and a real discrediting of war as a means of restoring rights. O'Connor does not deal with the shift in orientation, a shift in the direction of a theology of peace.

### Commentary on the 1982 Draft of a Pastoral Letter of the North American Bishops on the Morality of War

The American Catholic bishops, collectively and individually, have frequently addressed questions related to the morality of war. Many times their statements were, or were perceived to be, supportive of the position of the government. Often the bishops took a long time to determine what seemed fairly obvious to others. And, just as frequently, the bishops were criticized for saying anything at all about political, social, or economic policies of the government. Seldom were they praised for what they said. Nonetheless, the bishops do speak to public policy, and while what they say, or what is said on their behalf, may not please everyone or anyone, they maintain their duty to speak to public policy and to evaluate it in the light of the Catholic moral tradition.

This obligation is being acted on again in an examination of the morality of war, especially nuclear war and deterrence theory. Tentatively entitled "God's Hope in a Time of Fear," the various drafts of this pastoral letter have caused so much debate and so many differences of opinion have been manifest that the original publication date of November 1982 has been postponed until the spring or fall of 1983. Over seven hundred pages of comment have been submitted to the bishops and comments have appeared in various journals.[109] While some may feel that this delay is just another example of the bishops' avoiding hard decisions, it may also show that the bishops realize the seriousness of the issues and want more time to evaluate them.

This section will describe the process used to draft the pastoral letter thus far, will summarize the issues in the present draft, and will indicate some of the lines of the ongoing debate.

The draft of the pastoral letter had its beginning in the 1980 General Meeting of the American bishops. Archbishop Roach, then President of the National Council of Catholic Bishops, responded to Bishop Head's request, as Chairperson of the Social Development and World Peace Committee, that the NCCB leadership take responsibility for a discussion of the topic of the morality of war. Archbishop Roach appointed Archbishop Joseph Bernardin, now of Chicago, to chair an ad-hoc committee. Four other bishops—Fulcher, Gumbleton, O'Connor, and Reilly—were appointed. The United States Catholic Conference provided staffing in the persons of J. Bryan Hehir and Edward Doherty. Representatives from the Conference of Major Superiors of Men and the Leadership Conference of Women Religious Superiors were invited to be on the committee. Bruce M. Russett, professor of political science at Yale, and editor of *The Journal of Conflict Resolution,* was appointed to be the principal author.

Testimony was sought from various individuals: former government officials, moral theologians, Scripture scholars, representatives of Catholic peace organizations, conflict resolution specialists, retired military personnel, and members of the current administration. The bishops also discussed the first draft at their summer retreat in June 1982. Many of the bishops then distributed the draft to individuals in their dioceses for further comment. These comments, totaling over seven hundred pages, were collected at the USCC office in Washington and have been sent to the committee for evaluation and seem to be the primary reason for the delay in publication.

The process of developing the draft thus far has been criticized because representatives of various professional societies were not consulted, because the broader Catholic community was not consulted, except late and unofficially, and because the letter was developed too rapidly and without the necessary debate. These criticisms are somewhat accurate but they must be tempered by the fact that there was, for this letter, much broader consultation than had been done before. The list of consultants appended to the draft gives evidence of this. While that does not justify shortcomings in the procedure itself, nonetheless the procedure was relatively open and diverse and certainly sets a precedent for future consultation. Also the delay in publication will provide an opportunity for broader and more extensive consultation, as well as more extensive debate on the issues.

The second draft of the pastoral letter, available to many individuals and groups, will be the point of departure for the 1983 letter. This section will report on the main points of the draft to show where the bishops ended one stage of debate and what elements of the tradition were important to them.

Several elements of the tradition are brought together: the priority of peace and non-violence, and, consequently, the need to justify violence; the legitimate right, on the part of individuals and nations, to defend themselves with violent means if necessary, though there are limits to these; the use of the just war theory both to test the projected use of violence and to evaluate the means used; a commendation of pacifism, but a rejection of it as obligatory for all at the present time.

The just war theory is used as the primary methodology in the draft, but the bishops make several critical clarifications which take into account many of the teachings on the morality of war within the last decade. For example, the bishops explicitly limit the right intention in undertaking war for self-defense or the defense of others. While this can be traced to some themes in the teachings of Pius XII, this teaching is a helpful clarification of the just war theory for our time.

The draft also focuses on the principle of proportionality. Included in this moral calculus are the "demands of mobilizing a nation: economic burdens, the restructuring of basic human rights and freedoms, and the possible perversion of its own moral and spiritual values in the heat of conflict." (Draft, p. 15.) Frequently the effect of waging war has not been a part of its moral evaluation, and this teaching requires taking this significant dimension into account. Recent teaching has focused on the problem of who bears the cost of war, and the bishops have wisely and correctly pointed to a potential major consequence of war: the economic and spiritual destruction of the "victor." For frequently enough, when waging war, the side defined as "in the right" takes on the characteristics and behavior that led them to define the other group as "the enemy." An examination of propaganda material and the behavior of both the military and governments of warring nations reveals the high moral cost of waging war. The bishops are very correct in defining as morally relevant these internal costs of war.

Discrimination is another principle of the theory that the bishops single out for comment. This principle demands that "the lives of non-combatants not be taken directly. The lives of prisoners of war must be respected, and non-combatant civilians may not be directly attacked." (Draft, pp. 16–17.) Again, while presenting nothing new, this teaching highlights an important element of the calculation of the morality of means used in war. The reiteration of this teaching is important in particular in an age which tries to hide the horror of war by neutralizing language and attempting to reduce casualties to statistics. A counter-city strategy may make decision-making sound easier, but it ultimately cannot hide the moral outrage of the destruction of those individuals who live in these cities. Nor can the destruction of tens or hundreds of thousands of people be casually dismissed as "foreseen but unintended." As the letter clearly states, "Justice demands that those who do not make war not have war made on them." (Draft, p. 17.)

The bishops then go on, in the third section of the draft, to state the essence of their moral framework for the evaluation of war.

First, nuclear weapons or other weapons of mass destruction may not, under any circumstances, be used to destroy population centers in other predominantly civilian targets. Second, there is no perception of any situation in which any initiation of nuclear war—however restricted—can be condoned. In particular, non-nuclear attacks must be deterred by other than nuclear means. Third, the objections against the use of nuclear weapons against civilian targets and the initiation of nuclear war apply equally to the threat of such use. Fourth, in a recognition of moral pluralism, people of good will may differ as to whether nuclear weapons may be used under any circumstances. Fifth, the bishops recognize that if they reject any use of nuclear weapons, then they would have to face the question of whether it is permissible to continue to possess them. Sixth, the bishops hold a marginally justifiable deterrent policy.

Within this framework, summarily presented, there are several significant and highly controversial issues. The first has to do with the second principle which prohibits the initiation of nuclear war and using nuclear weapons to deter non-nuclear attacks. One dimension of these moral problems has to do with the development of counterforce weapons and weapons systems deployed in Europe which are capable of hitting Moscow in fewer than ten minutes. These weapons have initiated discussions of "launch on warning" policy. While theoretically functioning as a deterrence, such strategy may in fact provoke a nuclear war. Thus that which was intended to deter actually initiates. Another problem has to do with the use of "theater weapons," nuclear warheads which, because they are small, can be used strategically on the battlefield during conventional battles. Is it in any way realistic to think that this use of nuclear weapons can be contained? Is there any meaningful way to argue that the damage to civilian population centers is indirect and unintended? And can anyone believe that, once begun, the use of these weapons could be controlled or limited, especially if there was the slightest perception that one side was in danger of losing? The discipline required for such a policy is simply inconceivable, and my recommendation would be to prohibit any use of nuclear weapons. I cannot understand how there could be any meaningful possibility of victory in a nuclear exchange, how the destruction of population centers or civilian targets could be avoided, or how a battlefield exchange could be limited to only a few nuclear exchanges, giving one side the tactical advantage. Nuclear war, in my opinion, provides no hope of victory, violates proportionality, and is totally indiscriminate.

Second, the teaching on the use of nuclear weapons is confusing and convoluted. After recognizing, as has been noted, that people of good will may differ on the use of nuclear weapons, the bishops state: "It is difficult for us to see how what may be legitimate in theory may be justifiable in practice." (Draft, p. 30.) It is unclear to me what this means. If an act can be justified, that means, I would think, that the act can be performed. If it is on the basis of moral theory or moral criteria that we justify acts, then in what meaningful sense can something be said to be justified in theory but not in practice? If something cannot be justified in practice, I think that means it is because the practice cannot be justified by the moral theory used. Therefore the act should be prohibited.

The letter argues that if nuclear weapons can be used at all, they can be used only after they have been used against our country or our allies and then only in a limited, discriminating manner against military targets. An argument is also made that the knowledge that the enemy's forces would be destroyed—even though its cities would not—could serve as an effective deterrent. This is not intended as a justification of a counter-force strategy—the destruction of the enemy is strategic force—because, assumedly, that is a morally prohibited first-strike position.

The major problem with this justification is that it makes no sense to threaten or destroy the enemy's army if the mode of attack is missles armed with nuclear warheads. In a nuclear exchange conventional forces would not be used until much later in the war, if indeed such a use is conceivable after nuclear exchanges. In this perspective, then, the only deterrent that makes sense is a counter-force one.

From my perspective, then, the one justification presented simply makes no sense either as a strategy or as a deterrent. The draft then states that "no use of nuclear weapons can be considered moral if even *indirectly* it would result in significant violation of the principle of discrimination." (Draft, p. 31. Emphasis in original.) Given what is reported about the targeting of our missiles and their "throw-power" I can think only of the *indiscriminate* use of nuclear weapons. The damage from the fallout—both short and long term— makes the word "discrimination" unthinkable with respect to nuclear weapons. Also the harm to non-combatants would simply be unacceptable. Thus I would argue that the moral principles held in this draft argue against any use of nuclear weapons whatsoever. The reasoning used to try to justify some use is so tortured and strained that my sense is that the intent is to prohibit the use of nuclear weapons, but not to say this explicitly.

Perhaps the most complex and controversial section is on deterrence theory. Part of the problem of this section has to do with complexity and, indeed, the unreality of deterrence theory itself. One can easily become lost in the thicket of language that comes from trying to keep track of threat and counter-threat, perceptions of threat and counter-threat, intention of use versus intention to make one think one intends to use, etc. Abstracting from the linguistic dilemma— which is significant for the moral debate—is the question that the draft of the pastoral letter focuses on: Is it moral to threaten to do that which may be immoral to do? Then, if it is immoral to threaten to use nuclear weapons, is it immoral to possess them? The basic moral justification is that possession and threats to use serve as a deterrent and thus prevent the actual use.

The justification of the use of nuclear weapons as a deterrent is based on testimony presented to the U.S. Senate by Cardinal Krol in 1979. The critical excerpt from the testimony is found in the second chapter. Briefly the argument is that while the use of strategic nuclear weapons and the declared intent to use them is wrong, the possession of nuclear weapons can be tolerated as the lesser of two evils. But this can be the case only as long as negotiations proceed to reduce nuclear stockpiles and to phase out nuclear deterrence altogether. The draft of the pastoral letter concurs with this judgment by saying that the deterrence relation between the United States and Russia is "objectively a sinful situation because of the threats implied in it and the consequence it has in the world." (Draft, p. 35.) Yet, prudentially, movement out of this objectively evil situation must be done carefully lest the balance of terror be upset and a move to reduce a threat actually cause a nuclear holocaust because of a misperception of intention.

In addition to the requirement that negotiations continue for deterrence policy to be tolerable, the draft of the pastoral letter sets out three others: preventing the development and deployment of destabilizing weapons systems on either side; reducing the amount of automation in the command and control systems, making them more open to human intervention; preventing the proliferation of nuclear weapons in the international system.

This teaching is not intended to bring comfort to those who support the deterrence theory and is, in the bishops' own understanding, a barely justifiable theory. I note here two comments about this section that challenge the structure of the argument.

First, Charles Curran has challenged the use of the concept of toleration, based on the assumption that the evil to be tolerated is the evil intention to threaten population centers.

> If this is the case, then here is an application of toleration
> different from that of the past. One is hereby tolerating
> one's *own* intention to do evil (threaten a population cen-
> ter). In tolerating prostitution and the separation of

Church and state, one did not tolerate one's own intention
to do evil. Tolerating one's own evil intention appears to be
a new proposal in Catholic ethical thought.[110]

If Curran's assumption about the content of the intention is correct, then the draft of the pastoral letter has to overcome a significant
obstacle in traditional Catholic morality. For Curran is correct in
that what was tolerated in the traditional theory was the situation
not intended or caused by the moral agent, but the one in which the
moral agent found himself or herself—for some good reason. Thus a
critical flaw is present in the attempt to justify what one must intend
to do to make deterrence theory operable.

David Hollenbach makes another approach to the moral analysis of deterrence theory. First, he argues that one must distinguish
between the intent to use nuclear weapons and the intent to deter
their use. On this basis, a "moral judgment on the intention behind
deterrence policies is therefore inseparable from an evaluation of the
reasonably predictable outcomes of diverse policy choices."[111] Only if
the policy will actually prevent use will it be a deterrent and have
moral legitimacy. This distinction helps to set up a cleaner analysis
of the policies alleged to deter.

Second, Hollenbach argues that Krol makes toleration depend
on two conditions: a continued Soviet threat which makes unilateral
disarmament more dangerous than continued possession, and the
risk of nuclear war being reduced through effective arms reduction.
Although Hollenbach recognizes the correctness of this position as
stated, he provides a set of much clearer criteria.

First, any new policy proposal must make nuclear war less
likely than the policies presently in effect rather than more
likely. Second, any new policy must increase the possibility
of arms reduction rather than decrease this possibility.[112]

These policies can help cut through the rhetoric of deterrence
language and proposals to help evaluate the actual effect of a policy.
Thus while a policy may have an arms control proposal with it, the
weapons systems contained in the package may in fact be more likely

to increase the possibility of nuclear war. The criteria can also help us break from the political popularity of a particular policy to make the moral issues more accessible. Thus while congruous with the Krol proposals, the Hollenbach criteria are more clear and focused in getting to the heart of the moral analysis of the deterrence issue: Does the policy actually deter or does it increase the risk of nuclear war?

Although the issues of the morality of nuclear war and deterrence are critical and require clear analysis and firm moral judgment, the bishops are wise to delay publication of the pastoral letter. Since the document will be a Church document, special attention must be given to the comments of the Church. No one expects the bishops to agree with everything that is said, few will expect that the bishops can resolve the moral tension within the Catholic community over the issues of pacifism and the just war theory, and even fewer expect a statement that will satisfy all.

But the delay will provide time for a more careful consideration of the issues, out of which some moral consensus may occur within the Catholic community on which the teaching on the morality of war may be based. I also hope the delay will provide time to develop greater clarity within the letter. While the content must be carefully explained, nonetheless the draft can be much improved by a more clear statement of the teaching and the avoidance of language that either confuses or seems to hedge. While clarity and simplicity will not resolve the many moral issues involved, they will help us to know how and why the bishops want us to mature and develop as a Catholic community. The debate on the morality of nuclear weapons will obviously continue after the publication of the letter, but we will all benefit from a clear statement of principle from the bishops.

**Summary**

This overview of several orientations within the Catholic Church indicates both the tension and the promise of current debates on war and peace. On the one hand, some bishops are using the just war theory as a means of articulating a traditional orientation toward war and peace. On the other hand, other bishops are adopting a

much more prophetic orientation and using that as a means to critique the status quo. The bishops together hold a common goal of a
search for peace, but what is being demonstrated very interestingly in
the Catholic Church right now is the difference of methods with respect to how one goes about achieving that goal. I wish to turn now
to an examination of the new status of the examination of the question of war and peace.

# 5
# Peace and War . . .
# The State of the Question

### The Signs of the Time

One of the many things that Vatican Council II called for was looking at the question of war with an entirely new attitude. Part of the problem in dealing with this charge is to understand what attitude it is that we should use to re-examine war. In regard to the traditional just war theory, are we to use the categories of non-violence or pacifism, or must we step beyond both of these and use some other orientation to evaluate war? I think that part of the tension and problematic of the charge of Vatican II is easily discerned by recalling the statements of the different bishops. If one looks at the statements by Cardinal Cooke and Bishop O'Connor, one sees an evaluation of war in our age within the traditional categories of the just war theory. My evaluation of this orientation is that it produces a very narrow analysis of the issues. In my opinion, data about the military and the reality of nuclear war seem to be squeezed into an extremely narrow framework that can barely accommodate the issues at hand. This orientation also seems to rely tremendously on the use of ecclesiastical and civil authority and always conveys the impression that the wars in which our nation is involved are just wars. In many ways this orientation, which is by no means unique to the two authors I have cited, seems to be leading to the same tired old questions and to the same tired old answers. They get us nowhere and we remain enmeshed in the bowels of the war machine and in danger of destruction. The traditional orientation of the just war seems to give us no escape or relief from the terror of our times.

The questions raised by the just war theory are important. The theory has been used with great profit throughout the centuries to analyze the conduct of nations and soldiers within a particular war. The problem today, however, is that our situation has so dramatically changed with the advent of nuclear weapons that one must ask, or at least wonder, whether or not the reality of nuclear warfare has literally exploded the boundaries of the just war theory so that it can no longer be used in a constructive fashion. I think that we will profit greatly by continuing to use and ask the questions raised by the just war theory. But at a certain point the theory itself breaks down in the presence of the magnitude of the problems that we have.

The writings of Matthiesen and Hunthausen offer suggestions for approaching war in a new way. Whether or not this orientation will prove useful remains to be proven. I do think it is important to attend to some of the issues raised by these bishops in their statements as at least evidence of a new kind of thinking about war that may help us to escape the legalism of the just war theory and a kind of determinism in thinking about national defense and security.

## A Theology of Peace

The new orientation suggests that peace be the beginning premise rather than the conclusion of one's methodology. By this I mean that one must engage in the process of developing a theology of peace so that one may be working actively toward establishing structures in society and relationships among people that will help insure peace rather than see peace only as the end product of armed conflict. The state of affairs produced by deterrence and the arms race may not be active conflict, at least at the present moment, but one would hardly describe it as a state of peace because of the tensions and anxiety that the structure itself produces both nationally and internationally. Thus a primary part of a shift in attitude or a re-evaluation of war would require that we begin with peace as a premise rather than as a conclusion.

*The Moral Problem of Preparing for War*

We need to begin thinking of how deterrence strategy affects our lives. Rather than looking at proportionality of means and conducting a harm/benefit analysis or evaluating the status of non-combatants, I think that the bishops, for example, are beginning to focus on the extreme amounts of radical disruption that even the preparation for war causes. Matthiesen refers to the destruction of crop land, the uprooting of families, the depletion of water supply, and the expansion of services to fulfill short term needs, a situation that leads to long term disruption of the work force. Such a moral analysis establishes the priorities to determine how we will conduct our national defense. If it is important that we accept the sacrifices and the disruption of our daily lives required for national defense and security, why do we not accept that peacemaking will also require similar sacrifices and disruption of our lives? We need to recognize that this may be a price that we as Christians need to pay for establishing the structures of peace.

*A Theological Means of Evaluating War*

We need a theological basis as the new means of evaluating war. Hunthausen provides one orientation that helps to ground a theology of peace. As mentioned earlier, he uses the Gospel of Mark with its call to renounce self, take up the cross, and follow Jesus as the touchstone of this orientation. Hunthausen says that in our day we must think of the concrete and practical ways in which we need to take up the cross. He suggests that taking up the cross meant in Jesus' time being willing to die at the hands of political authorities for the truth of the Gospel. In our time he asserts that taking up the cross might require unilateral nuclear disarmament:

> I believe that one obvious meaning of the cross is unilateral disarmament. Jesus' acceptance of the cross rather than the sword raised in his defense is the Gospel's statement of unilateral disarmament. We are called to follow. Our security as people of faith lies not in demonic weapons which

threaten all life on earth. Our security is in a loving, caring God. We must dismantle our weapons of terror and place our reliance on God.

While there may and can be legitimate disagreement on that specific interpretation of the cross in our age, Hunthausen correctly requires that we begin translating specific elements of the Gospel message that stands behind traditional Christianity into ways of living that will promote peace. He concludes his statement by saying: "God alone is our salvation, through the acceptance in each of our lives of a non-violent cross-suffering love." By each individual's searching for what that means and by having the Church as an institution committed to looking for that kind of non-violent love, a way to peace is established as a premise and not as a conclusion.

## Medical Consequences of Nuclear War

An important orientation for the moral evaluation of nuclear war is being provided by the Society of Physicians for a Social Responsibility (PSR). A relatively new group, their orientation is to provide medical documentation of the consequences of nuclear warfare and to analyze and evaluate the implications of nuclear warfare for the health care system. The important contribution that these individuals are making, in addition to a witness for peace by a group of professionals, is to critique the claim that we can survive a nuclear war. The medical and scientific data that these physicians are providing suggest that our health care system is simply inadequate to deal with the aftermath of a nuclear war. No matter how well equipped a city may be in terms of hospitals and physicians, there simply will be neither the personnel nor resources to care adequately for all the people who will be seriously injured in a nuclear war, assuming, of course, that they survive the attack. Second, PSR makes us come to terms with the short and long term consequences of high doses of radiation exposure which follow a nuclear explosion. Again, the point they make is that while indeed there may be survivors after a nuclear war, eventually these individuals too will succumb to radiation sickness and die a very slow and painful death.

The critical message that this group is giving is that nuclear war is not winable because there will be no survivors. The resources that we have are inadequate to treat people and the consequences of such high level doses of radiation will cause massive damage to both the population and the resources of the earth. Those who may survive would wish that indeed they had died immediately.

The important orientation that PSR provides is the suggestion that a war waged with nuclear weapons simply cannot be won. And while this indeed is one of the tests of the just war theory, nonetheless I think that PSR is going beyond this in terms of a significantly critical evaluation of the health care resources of our country and their limitations with respect to caring for the survivors of a nuclear war. The issue is not simply: Can we win the war or not. It is: Will there be survivors? The answer is "no." Again such knowledge should begin to lead us to think in different directions for our national security and to take steps to insure that we will not be responsible for the destruction of humanity and our planet as well.

Another motivation PSR gives to resist nuclear war is the protection of our children. This is something that has been alluded to in different official texts from the Catholic Church as well as other Churches. It is important that a group of professionals has also raised the question in terms of the enlightened self-interest that should motivate one in trying to preserve the life of one's child. One of the most unnatural things that can happen is the death of a child. There is a sense that it is not fitting, that a future was snuffed out before it could begin. Consequently the death of a child is a genuine tragedy. Yet what are we doing by manufacturing more and more nuclear weapons? We are guaranteeing the destruction, the untimely end of our children. Self-interest and the parental instinct for preserving the life of a child should be ample motivation for a reevaluation of nuclear war.

## War and Christian Values

Another orientation toward thinking about war and peace from a new perspective comes from Eileen Egan who suggests that war reverses the most basic Christian concepts and values, especially as these relate to the Beatitudes and the corporal works of mercy. She points out that during the time of war, instead of visiting the sick

we dramatically increase the number of sick by shooting and bombing individuals. Instead of feeding the hungry, we defoliate forests
and fields to guarantee that people cannot eat. We take acres and
acres out of use as productive land so that they can be used as battle-
fields. Instead of burying the dead, we bomb cemeteries.

Many will say that this is the nature of war, but I think that
Egan's response must be taken seriously: as Christians, we don't do
that. We have other values that are more important. We have another vision that we are following and that vision prohibits us from con-
tradicting our deepest values and virtues which are important to us.
When we realize that participation in war makes us act in ways that
are utterly inappropriate and would produce cries of horror in other
circumstances and that also basically contradict our Christian virtues, then I think we might see war from a different perspective and
recognize that it serves to destroy not only life but also the qualities
that make life important.

## The State of the Question

In this section I wish to present several elements that I think are
present with respect to how the issue of war and especially the theory
of the just war doctrine are being discussed today.

### Problems with the Concept of the Just War

One problem is that war is no longer as contained an enterprise
with relatively reversible consequences. In the past, wars have been
limited fairly much to the territories of the belligerent nations, and
even though the effects of the war continue in the wounded veterans,
retirement benefits, displaced families and payments of loans for the
conducting of the war, such effects are essentially finite. Such is not
the case with nuclear war. Once a high level of radioactivity is released into the atmosphere, its effects endure for years and the health
and ecological consequences of this will be incredible. War can no
longer be limited and its effects cannot be reversed.

Traditionally war has been waged only between a few nations.
Even though the last major wars were described as world wars, still
only a relatively few of the nations of the world were involved. This

situation will also change in the event of a nuclear war. Although only two or three nations may actually deploy nuclear weapons, the entire world will be involved and its fate will be at stake because of the dangers from radioactive fallout. While it was possible in the past to think of war affecting primarily only those nations who were waging it, this is no longer viable because of the consequences of nuclear war.

Third, many people are beginning to have serious problems with the disproportionate amount of money that must be allocated to the military to continue building and deploying ever more lethal weapon systems. The problem is not so much allocating money for the defense of the nation; the problem is a genuine mortgaging of the social well-being of the nation so that more and more armaments may be built. Many people have already experienced serious disruptions in their lives because of the transfer of funds from entitlement programs to the defense budget. These increases are projected for many years to come and will continue to cause serious problems. Given this set of priorities for defense spending, we may find ourselves in the ironic situation of being the best defended nation in the world but having nothing worth defending because the quality of life has utterly disappeared.

### The Critique of the Just War Theory

Serious questions are also being raised about the theoretical structure by which wars are evaluated. In addition to questioning the viability of war itself, the theory by which war has traditionally been justified within Catholicism is also undergoing critique.

(a.) The Right To Conduct War (Jus ad bellum)

One of the major problems with the just war theory has to do with a nation's declaring a war. International politics have become so complex that it is difficult to disentangle the interests of one nation from another. Also there is no disinterested authority to adjudicate among the different nations so that one can know whether a right or an interest is being violated. International politics are presently so complex that the rights and interests of one nation cannot be seen apart from the similar rights of other nations.

A second problem with the right to declare war comes from the traditional postulate that the war must be declared by a competent authority. If a nuclear war were to begin or if a nation were to wish to initiate a first strike, there may be no time to consult with the traditional center of authority within the government. In our country this means the Congress. If the United States were the subject of a nuclear attack, we would only have a few moments within which to decide whether or not to retaliate, and Congress clearly could not be consulted. If we wished to initiate a first strike, consulting Congress to obtain its authority to declare war would take away all of the advantages of a first strike. Thus war would be declared either as a consequence of seeing another country's weapons coming at us or to gain the advantages connected with a first strike.

Third, another traditional criterion was that victory had to be a reasonable prospect. This criterion has undergone the most serious critique because in the event of a nuclear war there is no victory for anyone since the whole world will eventually be destroyed from radioactive fallout. If one side in a war uses a nuclear weapon, it is highly unlikely that another side will exercise restraint and will more than likely respond at least in kind. Once the nuclear exchange begins there can be no victory; there can only be the ashes of defeat, the destruction of the entire planet through radioactive fallout.

(b.) Duties in the Conducting of War (Jus in bello)

Many problems occur when one considers the traditional moral rules for the conducting of war.

How, for example, does one speak of proportionality with radioactivity? There really is no proportionate dose of radioactivity, especially when one takes into account the levels of radioactivity that nuclear weapons will release into the ecosphere.

How can one speak of the immunity of non-combatants when the radioactivity will be released into the atmosphere and distribute itself all over the earth, falling upon those who may not even know that a war has begun? Radioactive fallout is not selective in terms of how it falls to the earth. Thus no one—no matter what he or she believes, knows, or feels about a war that has begun elsewhere—has any possibility of being a non-combatant.

A final issue with respect to the traditional criteria for evaluating duties in the conducting of war is that primary targets are not exclusively or primarily military targets—they are cities. Even though one can argue that many nuclear installations are around major urban areas and that therefore they are legitimate targets, this still does not take away the reality that part of a strategy of nuclear deterrence and nuclear war is to render unacceptable levels of civilian casualties on a particular nation. Thus one of the traditional rules is violated by making all of the citizens of a country hostage to the threat of destruction in a nuclear exchange.

These dimensions of how war is conducted in a nuclear age make it exceedingly difficult to speak of a just war in the traditional sense. While some would argue that the traditional concepts may still find legitimate application, many more are arguing that such an application is exceedingly more difficult to justify. Others, of course, argue that the points that I have made clearly demonstrate that the traditional theory of the just war is utterly useless.

## A New Direction

In this section I will indicate some elements I see that are part of a new evaluation of war. While I do not propose the following comments as a new just war theory, I think that these are ethical concerns that emerge out of contemporary discussions of war and peace and will form part of a new synthesis. At best, the just war theory is under radical critique and attempts to use it to justify nuclear war are meeting strong resistance. At worst, the theory has been proven to be inapplicable in today's society and consequently we are left adrift, not having an accessible and acceptable methodology for the analysis of nuclear war. I propose the following as elements to be taken into account as we work through a new synthesis.

### Perceptions of War

#### (a.) War as an International Event

War in today's society, especially nuclear war but also conventional war, will at some point involve the majority of the nations of the world. No one will be able to escape taking sides and all will be affected in terms of the diversion of resources to the warring nations, and, in the worst scenario, all will suffer the ravages of radioactive fallout from a nuclear exchange. In our contemporary situation, all the peoples of the earth equally will be victims of war. The land itself will be a victim because, having become radioactive, it will no longer be fruitful. It is in the interest of all nations to attempt to protect each other, their citizens, and the land and ecosphere that gives us life and nourishment. If we do not do this all may be lost.

### (b.) The Cost of War

As I mentioned before it is becoming more and more expensive to pay for war. This cost is not exclusively financial. More and more of our brightest scientists and engineers are using their talents for the production of weapons of destruction rather than using them for the development of technologies that will serve life. Not only our money, but our talent, our energy, and our creative thought serve war rather than life. The Reagan administration has put a higher priority on the military than on the human services that go to make life worth living. The major ethical problem is examining the priorities of our country and learning what those priorities say about us as a people. What will there be to defend if our nation is turned into a huge armed camp?

### (c.) The Consequences of Nuclear War

I have alluded several times to the enormous consequences that will occur if there is a nuclear exchange. High levels of radioactivity will guarantee that there will be a few immediate survivors of the nuclear exchange, and the continued presence of radioactivity in the environment will guarantee that both the earth and the people who have survived the first exchange will eventually die hideous deaths because of various illnesses produced by the high levels of radioactivity. Those who survive may be the most unfortunate of all because they are guaranteed an extremely painful death. It is this reality that we must squarely face because there is a fair amount of argumentation that a nuclear war can be survivable. One must look at the consequences of a nuclear exchange and realize that in the long run there can be no survivors because a nuclear exchange will wipe out all of the physical and social structures that are necessary for human life to survive. Even for those individuals who survive the initial exchange, there will be no place to go and no one to care for them. There will be no food, shelter, or energy. Life as we have known it will have vanished, and in a relatively short time the survivors will also vanish because they will not be able to withstand the ravages of the continued presence of radioactive materials in the environment.

## Methods of Analysis

### (a.) Prophetic

One of the clear orientations emerging out of many contemporary Catholic discussions of war and peace is a prophetic stance against the priorities of our country with respect to both national defense and its cost. Many bishops are recalling that a very important tradition within Christianity is the tradition of non-violence, the moral imperative of loving one's enemies. Connected with this we may also refer to the tradition of the suffering servant who bears the burdens of the nation so that the nation may live and prosper.

While not focusing on the specific strategic and defense-oriented concepts that have been so much of a part of the just war theory, the new prophetic orientation focuses critically on the question of what kind of a people will we become if we continue to act the way we have been. This question is extremely important to answer because it involves an examination of our priorities and of the kind of society we wish to have. Such a question ought to be at the heart of the moral analysis of war from a Christian perspective because of the vocation to which we have been called and because of the model provided for us by Jesus.

### (b.) Analytic

In addition to the prophetic dimension there is also a substantive analytic orientation being developed to examine the question of the morality of war in our day. However this orientation does not come at the question from the same stance that the traditional just war theory has. Rather, this analytic orientation is looking at the cost of war and the consequences of war in terms of the psychological, physical, and resource dimensions.

The issue here is examining what will become of us as we continue to invest more and more resources into preparations for war. Many are asking whether it is appropriate to mortgage the future of our youth as well as the security of our older citizens for the monies needed to prepare for war. The resource allocation question is becoming much more critical because it is becoming more apparent that our resources are finite and cannot continue to be squandered in the way we have been doing.

Psychologically, we need to attend to what we will become if we continue to live under the spectre of the imminent threat of total annihilation. While this threat may not be as apparent a problem as the issue of resource allocations, nonetheless the issue is important because it produces a wearing down of the spirit, a background of numbness which can only lead to the psychological debilitation of everyone. The resource problem also feeds into this psychological dimension because a continued decrease in resources leads to a fear of scarcity, to a selfishness of spirit that puts one's own interest above the common good. Such an orientation works counter to the American tradition of focusing on needs of others and concern with the good of other individuals.

There is also the problem of the actual physical cost of war itself. A variety of revised cost projections are released almost daily. These figures range into the trillions of dollars over the next five years to support the war effort. It is quite accurate to say that a substantive amount of the budgetary projections for the military has to do with both the paying of health and retirement benefits and other associated costs to veterans and the maintaining of the armaments that we already have. Nonetheless large amounts of money are being spent for the development of new weapons of destruction as well as for the re-establishment of a biological and chemical warfare potential. It is clear that the budgetary allocations for the military are growing at a rapid rate while the money available for entitlement programs and for social needs is used to pay for war. The ultimate irony of continued spendings for the military and decreased spendings for social welfare would be that of America as an inviolable fortress but with nothing but decay to protect.

This analytic method of evaluating war focuses on issues that traditionally have not been brought into the just war theory and look more toward the issue of the actual costs of preparing for war and what that will do to us as a nation both culturally and individually. Attention to issues such as these put the issue of the preparing for war and its waging in a much different perspective and give us a new lens through which to see the reality of warfare.

**To Walk in the Way of Peace**

One of the critical elements in this new orientation is the proposing of a theology of peace. I will indicate four qualities that I think must be part of that orientation, although they are by no means exhaustive.

*A Spirit of Internationalism*

One quality we need to develop among all people is a spirit of internationalism. From a practical point of view internationalism is already a reality because we all are mutually dependent on each other to care for and preserve the goods of this world. We are all bound to our planet by a delicate ecocycle, and the only way to preserve our resources and ourselves is to look to the good of all.

From a theological point of view a spirit of internationalism is a very deep part of Christianity. Christianity, as well as other religions, proclaims that God is the God of all. Since all are created in the image of God, all are equally brothers and sisters. Such an orientation leads very naturally to a spirit of concern for each other and for a way of seeing one another that can transcend race and nationalism.

*A Spirit of Trust*

Trust is a quality that is hard to develop because typically it must be earned rather than presumed. Yet, again, if we are to survive we must begin practicing the kinds of relationships that will lead to trust, and we must begin to work with each other in the expectation that we all are trustworthy. Such an attitude is related to the spirit of internationalism and is based on the reality that our common good is at stake. What we need to do is to begin engaging in actions that will promote the common good and that will lead us to know that we can indeed work with and trust each other.

*A Spirit of Freedom*

One of the most valued qualities of human life, culturally, politically, and religiously, is a spirit of freedom. This spirit allows each human individual to flourish by giving that individual the opportunity to bring forth what is best in himself or herself so that these gifts can be shared with the community. From a political perspective, freedom provides the social structures which allow and encourage all members of a society to promote the freedom of each other and to respect what is brought forth as what is best in the individual.

From the Christian perspective the truest freedom that we have comes from the release from sin and allows us to walk in trust and joy with those we meet along our way. It is also important to remember from a religious perspective that freedom is not only a freedom from sin but is also a freedom for action, a freedom for developing those qualities of life that can enhance us and bring out the best in us.

## A Spirit of Love

The gift of love is, from a Christian perspective, the most unique and precious gift that God has given to us, most especially revealed in the gift of Jesus. In his life, Jesus revealed a tremendous love, openness, and acceptance of the men and women that he met. It is this tradition that he has handed on to us, a tradition which he acted out in the healing of the sick, the sharing of meals with sinners, the washing the feet of his disciples, and his acceptance of death as a means of saving the world.

Such an example of love calls us to respond in a similar way in our own lives. This example tells us that suffering is a part of love, that efforts must be made to encourage and bring about a spirit of love, and that the offering of love is frequently a gift that is refused. Yet the deepest instinct of Christianity is to ask that this gift continue to be offered and to be put into practice in all of the actions of our lives.

The vocation of love that is given to us as Christians is best summed up in the prayer that Saint Francis left us. It is both a prayer and a plan for peace.

**Lord, make me an instrument of your peace.**
**Where there is hatred, let me sow love;**
**Where there is injury, pardon;**

Where there is doubt, faith;
Where there is despair, hope;
Where there is darkness, light;
Where there is sadness, joy.

O Divine Master, grant that I may seek not so much
To be consoled as to console;
To be understood as to understand;
To be loved as to love;
For it is in giving that we receive;
It is in pardoning that we are pardoned;
And it is in dying that we are born to eternal life.

# Notes

1. A good survey of the issue of war and peace in world religions, on which some of the following material is based, is John Ferguson, *War and Peace in the World Religions.* New York: Oxford University Press, 1978.

2. For an extended treatment, see Roland Bainton, *Christian Attitudes Towards War and Peace.* New York: Abingdon, 1960.

3. *Ibid.,* pp. 67–68.

4. St. Augustine, *The City of God,* Book 19, Chapter 17.

5. St. Thomas Aquinas, *Summa Theologica* 2a–2ae, XI, I. Quoted in *Saint Thomas Aquinas: Philosophical Texts,* edited by Thomas Gilby. New York: Oxford University Press, 1960, p. 348.

6. Francisco De Vitoria, *De Jure Belli,* 25. Quoted in LeRoy Walters, "A Historical Perspective on Selective Conscientious Objection," *Journal of the American Academy of Religion,* XLI (June 1973), p. 205.

7. Francisco De Vitoria, *De Jure Belli,* 467.60. Quoted from the *Catholic Tradition of the Law of Nations,* The Catholic Association for International Peace. New York: Paulist Press, 1934, p. 106.

8. Francisco Suarez, *De Legibus ac de Deo Legislatore,* Chapter 13, Section 1, Paragraph 7. Quoted in the *Catholic Tradition of the Law of Nations, op. cit.,* p. 108.

9. Material in this section is based on William F. Roemer, John Tracy Ellis, *et al., The Catholic Church and Peace Efforts,* The Catholic Association for International Peace. New York: Paulist Press, 1934.

10. Pope Pius XI, *Peace Statements of Recent Popes.* Washington: National Catholic Welfare Conference, 1930, p. 6.

11. Pius XII, "The Twofold Duty of All Christians," 1948 Christmas Message. Quoted in *Major Addresses of Pope Pius XII,* Volume 2, edited by Vincent Yzermans. Saint Paul: Northcentral Publishing Company, 1961, p. 124.

12. Pius XII, "Conditions for a New World Order," Christmas Message of 1940. Quoted in Yzermans, *op. cit.,* p. 37.

13. Pope Pius XII, "Characteristics of the Christian Will for Peace," 1948 Christmas Message. Quoted in Yzermans, *op. cit.,* p. 124.

14. *Ibid.,* p. 125.

15. Pope Pius XII, "International Medical Law." Quoted in Yzermans, Volume II, p. 262.

16. Pope Pius XII. "Communism and Democracy." 1956 Christmas Message. Quoted in Yzermans, *op. cit.,* p. 225.

17. *Loc. cit.*

18. Pope John XXIII, *Pacem in Terris,* n. 127.

19. Pope Paul VI, *Populorum Progressio,* n. 31.

20. Pope Paul VI, "If You Wish Peace, Defend Life," 1976 World Peace Day Message. *The Pope Speaks,* 22 (1977), p. 42.

21. Pope Paul VI, "Toward A Balance of Trust," 1978 Message to the United Nations. *The Pope Speaks,* 23 (1978), p. 278.

22. Pope John Paul II. *Redemptor Hominis,* n. 16.

23. Pope John Paul II. "The Dignity of the Human Person Is the Basis of Justice and Peace," 1979 Address to the United Nations. *The Pope Speaks,* 24 (1979), p. 310.

24. *Gaudium et Spes,* n. 80.

25. *Ibid.*

26. *Ibid.*

27. *Ibid.,* n. 79.

28. *Ibid.*

29. *Ibid.*

30. *Ibid.*

31. *Ibid.,* n. 78.

32. *Ibid.,* n. 79.

33. "The Holy See and Disarmament." *The Pope Speaks,* 22 (1977), p. 246. Italics in original.

34. *Ibid.,* p. 247. Italics in original.

35. *Human Life in Our Day,* 1968 Pastoral Letter of the American Bishops. The United States Catholic Conference, Chapter 2.

36. *Ibid.*

37. *Ibid.*

38. *Ibid.*

39. *Ibid.*

40. *To Live As Christ Jesus,* 1976 Pastoral Letter of the American Bishops. The United States Catholic Conference.

41. "The Gospel of Peace and the Danger of War," A United States Catholic Conference Pamphlet.

42. John Cardinal Krol, testimony for the United States Catholic Commission before the United States Senate Foreign Relations Committee. Quoted from "The Nuclear Threat: Reading the Signs of the Times," Office of International Justice and Peace. Washington, D.C.: The United States Catholic Conference, p. 9.

43. *Ibid.*

44. *Ibid.,* pp. 9–10. Italics in original.

45. Reverend J. Bryan Hehir, testimony for the United States Catholic Conference before the House Committee on Armed Services in FY 81 Appropriations Authorization Act, March 14, 1980. Washington, D.C.: The United States Catholic Conference.

46. John Ford, S.J., "The Morality of Obliteration Bombing," *Theological Studies.* Volume 5 (September 1944), p. 267.

47. John Ford, S.J., "Current Moral Theology and Canon Law," *Theological Studies* 2 (December 1941), p. 551.

48. *Ibid.,* p. 556. Italics in original.

49. John Ford, S.J., "Moral Theology, 1942," *Theological Studies* 3 (December 1942), p. 586. Italics in original.

50. Ford, "The Morality of Obliteration Bombing," *op. cit.,* p. 267.

51. *Ibid.,* p. 281.

52. *Ibid.,* p. 291.

53. *Ibid.,* p. 292.

54. *Ibid.,* p. 294.

55. *Ibid.,* p. 302.

56. *Ibid.,* p. 309.

57. Gerald Kelly, S.J., "Notes on Moral Theology, 1950," *Theological Studies* 12 (March 1951), p. 58.

58. Gerald Kelly, S.J. "Notes on Moral Theology, 1951," *Theological Studies* 13 (December 1952), p. 66.

59. John C. Murray, *We Hold These Truths.* Garden City, N.Y.: Image, 1964, p. 244.

60. *Ibid.,* pp. 249–50.

61. *Ibid.,* p. 258.

62. John C. Murray, "Conscience and the Just War." A Catholic Peace Fellowship Booklet.

63. Murray, *We Hold These Truths, op. cit.,* p. 255.

64. Paul Hanley Furfey, *The Mystery of Iniquity.* Milwaukee: The Bruce Publishing Company, 1944, p. 152.

65. Paul Hanley Furfey, *The Morality Gap.* New York: Macmillan, 1962, p. 73.

66. *Ibid.,* p. 30.

67. Furfey, *The Mystery of Iniquity, op. cit.,* p. 161.

68. Furfey, *The Morality Gap, op. cit.,* p. 139.

69. *Ibid.*

70. Patricia McNeal, *The American Catholic Peace Movement: 1928–1972.* New York: Arno Press, 1978, pp. 64–78.

71. William Miller, *A Harsh and Dreadful Love.* New York: Liveright, 1973, p. 160.

72. Gordon C. Zahn, editor, *The Nonviolent Alternative.* New York: Farrar, Straus and Giroux, 1980, p. 67.

73. *Ibid.,* p. 68.

74. *Ibid.,* pp. 34–35.

75. *Ibid.,* p. 88.

76. *Ibid.,* p. 89.

77. *Ibid.,* p. 84.

78. *Ibid.,* p. 85.

79. *Ibid.,* p. 161.

80. Daniel Berrigan, *The Bride.* New York: Macmillan, 1959.

81. Daniel Berrigan, S.J., *No Bars to Manhood,* Garden City, N.Y.: Doubleday, 1970, p. 107.

82. Daniel Berrigan, S.J., *The Trial of the Catonsville Nine.* Boston: Beacon Press, 1970.

83. J. Bryan Hehir, "The Just War Ethic and Catholic Theology: Dynamics of Change and Continuity," in *War or Peace: The Search for New Answers,* Thomas A. Shannon, editor. Maryknoll, N.Y.: Orbis Press, 1979, p. 22.

84. *Ibid.,* p. 27.

85. *Ibid.,* p. 32.

86. Charles Curran, *Politics, Medicine, and Christian Ethics.* Philadelphia: Fortress Press, 1973, p. 75.

87. *Ibid.,* p. 78.

88. *Ibid.,* p. 99.

89. Charles Curran, *American Catholic Social Ethics: Twentieth Century Issues.* University of Notre Dame Press. Forthcoming.

90. Among Zahn's major contributions are the following: *War, Conscience and Dissent.* New York: Hawthorn, 1967. *The Solitary Witness.* Boston: Beacon Press, 1964. *Another Part of the War: The Camp Simon Story.* Amherst: The University of Massachusetts Press, 1979.

91. Archbishop Joseph L. Bernardin. Report of the National Council of Catholic Bishops Ad Hoc Committee on War and Peace. Washington, D.C.: The United States Catholic Conference, 1981.

92. *Ibid.*

93. Cf. the full text of Bishop Pilla's statement for further development of this idea.

94. Archbishop John R. Quinn, "Instruments of Peace—Weapons of War." Boston: Daughters of Saint Paul, 1981, p. 10.

95. *Ibid.,* p. 11.

96. Bishop L. T. Matthiesen, Statement on the MX Missile System. Presented April 20, 1981. *West Texas Catholic,* May 3, 1981.

97. Bishop L. T. Matthiesen, Statement on the production and stockpiling of the neutron bomb. Presented August 23, 1981. *West Texas Catholic.*

98. Archbishop Raymond G. Hunthausen. "Faith and Disarmament." Speech delivered to the Pacific Northwest Synod for the Lutheran Church in America, June 12, 1981.

99. *Ibid.*

100. Archbishop Raymond G. Hunthausen, Speech to peace rally, sponsored by Nuclear Weapons Freeze Committee, October 24, 1981.

101. *Ibid.*

102. Archbishop Raymond G. Hunthausen, pastoral letter, January 28, 1982.

103. *Gaudium et Spes,* n. 79.

104. Terrence Cardinal Cooke, pastoral letter to Catholic chaplains of the armed services, p. 2. Italics in the original.

105. *Ibid.,* p. 4.

106. Bishop John J. O'Connor, *In Defense of Life.* Boston: Daughters of Saint Paul, 1981.

107. *Ibid.,* p. 65.

108. Ibid., pp. 28ff.

109. *National Catholic Reporter,* 2 July 1982, Vol. 18, No. 34. *Commonweal,* 13 August 1982, Vol. 109, No. 14.

110. Charles Curran, "A Complex Document For a Big Church." *Commonweal,* 13 August 1982, (Vol. 109, No. 14), p. 439.

111. David Hollenbach, S.J. "Nuclear Weapons and Nuclear War: The Shape of the Catholic Debate." Presented to the Fifth Annual Colloquium of Catholic Bishops and Catholic Scholars. P. 39. This essay will appear, in a slightly revised form, in *Theological Studies,* December 1982. My citation is from the original manuscript.

112. *Ibid.* pp. 40–43.

113. Hunthausen, Statement of June 12, 1981, *op. cit.*

114. *Ibid.*